INTERES
FACTS & S
THROUGHOUT
HISTORY
For Curious Kids!

WHAT IS THE FORBIDDEN CITY?

WHATS THE STORY OF LIEF ERIKSON?

WHO WERE THE SPARTA?

WHY DID WE BUILD PYRAMIDS?

FIVE MILE PUBLICATIONS

Contents

THE DINOSAUR AGE

The dinosaur age began around 300 million years ago and was a time when dinosaurs roamed the Earth. The continents were joined together in the beginning, but they started to break apart over time, creating new habitats for dinosaurs, separated by water. The dinosaur age is divided into three periods: the Triassic, Jurassic, and Cretaceous, each with different dinosaur species that thrived. Unfortunately, the dinosaur age ended when a massive asteroid hit the Earth around 65 million years ago, causing the extinction of the dinosaurs and many other plants and animals. Today, we continue to learn more about dinosaurs through the study of fossils.

The Dinosaur Age

Did You Know?

The word dinosaur comes from Greek and means 'terrible lizard'.

Extreme Sizes

Possibly the smallest dinosaur ever discovered is called the Microraptor, which was about the size of a modern-day chicken. It lived during the early Cretaceous period in what is now China. Despite its small size, the Microraptor was a fascinating creature with long, feathered wings on its arms and legs that allowed it to glide through the air.

On the other end of the spectrum, possibly the largest dinosaur ever discovered is the Argentinosaurus, which lived during the late Cretaceous period in what is now Argentina. The Argentinosaurus was a massive herbivorous dinosaur that could weigh up to 100 tons, which is equivalent to the weight of about 10 elephants! It was also about 100 feet long, which is as long as a basketball court.

Despite its enormous size, the Argentinosaurus was actually quite gentle, feeding on plants and using its long neck to reach high into the trees.

The Dinosaur Age

T-Rex

The T. Rex, short for Tyrannosaurus rex, was one of the most fearsome predators that ever lived during the dinosaur age. It was a large, two-legged dinosaur that lived during the late Cretaceous period, about 68 to 66 million years ago. One of the most distinctive features of the T. Rex was its enormous, sharp teeth, which were as big as bananas!

These massive teeth were perfectly adapted for crushing bones and tearing through flesh, allowing the T. Rex to take down even the largest of prey. In fact, scientists estimate that the T. Rex could bite with a force of up to 12,000 pounds per square inch, which is more than twice the bite force of a modern-day crocodile.

Despite its fearsome reputation, the T. Rex was actually a highly intelligent creature. It had an excellent sense of smell, which it used to track its prey over long distances, and its keen eyesight allowed it to spot potential threats from far away. The T. Rex was also capable of running at speeds of up to 20 miles per hour, which is impressive considering its large size and weight.

Clever Dinosaur

Believe it or not, some dinosaurs had a second brain in their tail! This second brain is known as the "caudal brain" and it was found in dinosaurs like the Stegosaurus and the Ankylosaurus. The caudal brain helped to regulate the tail's movements, allowing the dinosaur to keep its balance and make quick, accurate turns.

The caudal brain also helped the dinosaur to react quickly to danger. Because it was located at the base of the tail, it was closer to the dinosaur's feet and legs. This meant that it could send signals more quickly than the main brain, allowing the dinosaur to move out of harm's way faster!

Discovery

The first dinosaur fossil ever discovered was in 1824 by an English scientist named William Buckland, who was exploring the countryside near the town of Stonesfield in Oxfordshire, England.

At first, Buckland thought the fossil was from an ancient crocodile or lizard. But as he studied it more closely, he realized that it was something entirely new and different - a type of giant reptile that had lived millions of years ago during the dinosaur age. Buckland named this new creature Megalosaurus, and sparked a worldwide interest for finding fossils from other megalosauruses, or as they are called today, dinosaurs!

Vegetarians

Although some of the most iconic dinosaurs were carnivorous (meat-eating) predators, such as the T-Rex, it may come as a surprise that the majority of dinosaur species were actually herbivores (plant-eating), and they evolved a variety of adaptations to help them digest tough plants.

Some of the most well-known herbivorous dinosaurs include the Stegosaurus, Triceratops, and Brachiosaurus. These dinosaurs had large, flat teeth that were perfect for grinding and crushing plant matter. They also had long necks and specialized digestive systems that allowed them to extract as many nutrients as possible from their food. The brachiosaurus for example, had a neck as long as a telephone pole! Despite some of their enormous sizes, you would have likely been safe befriending a herbivorous dinosaur, since you would not get eaten!

Birds

It has been discovered that some dinosaurs did indeed have feathers, just like modern-day birds. Scientists believe that many of the dinosaurs that lived during the late Jurassic and early Cretaceous periods may have had some form of feather on their bodies! These feathers were likely used for a variety of purposes, such as insulation, display, or even flight. While many of the feathered dinosaurs were small and agile, some of the largest and most fearsome predators, such as the Velociraptor and the Tyrannosaurus Rex, may have also had feathers!

Imagine Living In The Dinosaur Age

The world during the dinosaur age was a very different place than it is today. The climate was much warmer and there were no cities or towns as we know them. Instead, the landscape was dominated by vast forests and swamps, which were home to a diverse range of plant and animal life.
If we were to venture into these wild areas as humans, we would have to be very careful, as there were many large and dangerous

predators roaming around! We might encounter massive herbivorous dinosaurs like the Brachiosaurus or Triceratops, which could easily crush us underfoot, or ferocious carnivores like the Tyrannosaurus Rex, which could tear us apart with its massive jaws and sharp teeth.

To survive in this dangerous world, we would have had to be very resourceful and adaptable. We might have had to build shelters out of natural materials like leaves, branches, and mud, and we would have had to hunt and gather our food in the wild. We would have had to rely on our instincts and knowledge of the environment to avoid danger and stay alive.

Triceratops

The Triceratops was a large herbivorous dinosaur that lived during the Late Cretaceous period, about 68 to 66 million years ago. One of the most distinctive features of this dinosaur was its large, bony frill that extended from the back of its head and covered its neck. This frill was adorned with a series of spikes and horns, which likely served as a means of defense against predators.

The Triceratops also had a very large head relative to its body size, which is what makes the fact that its head was one-third the size of its body so impressive. In fact, the head of the Triceratops was one of the largest and most heavily reinforced of any animal that has ever lived on land.

The skull of the Triceratops was incredibly thick and strong, with bones that were up to 10 inches (25 cm) thick in some places. This allowed the Triceratops to use its head like a battering ram, delivering powerful blows to any predator that dared to approach it.

Swift Thief

The Velociraptor was another famous dinosaur that was only about the size of a large turkey, and likely weighed only around 30 to 40 pounds (14 to 18 kg). However, what the Velociraptor lacked in size and strength, it made up for in speed and agility. This dinosaur was incredibly fast and agile, with long, powerful legs and sharp, curved claws that it used to latch onto and tear apart its prey, making the velociraptor probably just as deadly, if not more, than the T-rex.

The End

Dinosaurs went extinct around 65 million years ago, when a massive meteor crashed into Earth, into what is today Mexico, at over 40,000 mph! The asteroid impact was so powerful that it caused a global catastrophe, sending large amounts of dust and debris into the atmosphere. This debris blocked out the sun and caused a rapid cooling of the Earth's climate, which in turn led to a global disruption of the food chain. Without enough food to sustain them, many of the large herbivorous dinosaurs died out, and with them, the predators that relied on them for food also went extinct. The asteroid impact may have also caused massive wildfires and tsunamis, which further contributed to the destruction of the dinosaur's habitats. However, not all of the dinosaurs went extinct at the same time. Some smaller species of dinosaurs, such as birds, were able to survive and continue to thrive to this day. In fact, birds are considered to be the direct descendants of some of the smaller, feathered dinosaurs that lived directly before the meteor strike.

PREHISTORIC ERA

The prehistoric era was a time before written records, but we know about it from fossils, cave paintings, and artifacts. People were hunters and gatherers who used stone tools and fire, lived in caves or simple shelters, and later developed more advanced tools, domesticated animals, and grew crops. Agriculture and metalworking were important events that led to the growth of villages and cities. The prehistoric era lasted for millions of years, and humans evolved and developed new skills and technologies that allowed them to survive and thrive.

The Earliest Known Humans

Once upon a time, the world looked different, there were no humans on Earth. But over 2 million years ago, a new species called Homo Habilis, the first recorded humans evolved in East Africa. These early humans were small and had big brains for their size. They were also very clever, and figured out how to make stone tools to help them survive. This was the beginning of human history!

The First Stone Tools

One day, around 2.5 million years ago, a group of Homo habilis humans were searching for food. They stumbled upon some stones and began to experiment with them, hitting them against each other to see what would happen. To their surprise, they discovered that they could shape the stones into tools, like knives and scrapers, which made it easier to hunt and prepare food. This was the beginning of stone tool-making, which would become an important part of human history.

Living Here As A Child

Living in the prehistoric era as a child would be very different from our lives today. You would likely live in a small tribe or family group and spend most of your time hunting and gathering food, making clothing and tools from natural materials like animal hides and rocks, and taking care of your younger siblings.

You would live in a cave or a simple shelter made from branches, leaves, and animal skins. You would sleep on the ground or on a pile of leaves or grass, and your parents might make a fire for warmth and light. You would eat mostly meat, fish, fruits, and vegetables, and you would have to hunt or gather your food every day. You might help your parents by gathering berries, nuts, or fruits or by fishing in a nearby river or lake. You would learn how to make your own tools, such as spears and arrows, by watching your parents and older siblings. You might also learn how to make clothing by weaving animal hides or by using plant fibers to make baskets or mats. You would play games with your siblings and other children in your tribe, such as running and jumping contests, and you might even make your own toys.

The First Humans to Leave Africa

Around 1.8 million years ago, a group of Homo Erectus humans decided to leave their home in Africa and explore other parts of the world. They walked for miles and miles, across deserts, through forests, and over mountains, until they finally reached new lands. They were the first humans to migrate out of Africa and would go on to populate much of the world.

The Oldest Known Cave Paintings

Deep inside a cave in Spain called the Maltravieso cave, a group of people gathered around a fire. They had a special gift: the ability to create art. They picked up their tools and began to paint on the walls of the cave, using pigments made from crushed rocks and minerals. The paintings they created, which included red hand stencils are around 60,000 years old and are some of the oldest known examples of human art.

The Woolly Mammoth

In the frozen tundras of the Ice Age, a giant creature roamed the earth. It was the woolly mammoth, a species of elephant that was about the same size as modern elephants, but had long, shaggy fur to keep it warm. These magnificent beasts were well adapted to the cold, with special features like small ears and a hump of fat on their backs to help them survive in the harsh environment.

The First Musical Instrument

In a cave in Germany, a group of people gathered around a fire. One person picked up a bone, found a hole and decided to blow into it, creating a beautiful sound. This was the first known musical instrument, a flute made from bone, and it is over 40,000 years old.

Humanity's First Pet

A group of people noticed that there were some wolves hanging around their campsite. Instead of chasing them away, as others normally do, they decided to feed them and befriend them. Over time, the wolves began to trust the humans and follow them, and the humans began to rely on the wolves for protection and help with hunting. This was the beginning of domestication, and the first domesticated animal was the dog, which was domesticated from wolves around 15,000 years ago.

Neanderthals

Possibly evolving from the Homo Erectus, there were another type of human called Neanderthals. They lived in caves and hunted animals for food. What's interesting is that they actually had bigger brains than we do! This means they were very smart and were able to make tools and weapons to help them survive.

The First Pottery

Imagine living in a world without bowls or plates to eat from! Thousands of years ago, people didn't have these things either. But during the Neolithic period, which was a time when people started farming and living in one place, they figured out how to make pottery. They would take clay from the ground and shape it into bowls, cups, and other things they needed!

Not Your Typical Sloth

Have you ever heard of a sloth? They're those cute animals that move really slowly and look kind of lazy. But a long time ago, there were giant sloths that lived in the

Americas during the Ice Age. They were as big as an elephant and had huge, curved claws that they used to dig for food. Unfortunately, they are no longer around.

Ancient Australia

Australia is a big island that is surrounded by water. But a long time ago, people still managed to get there! The first humans to settle in Australia were called the Aboriginal Australians. They arrived there around 60,000 years ago and they were able to survive in the harsh environment by hunting and gathering food.

A Wheely Good Invention

The first known wheel was invented in Mesopotamia around 3,500 BCE. At the time, people used to walk everywhere they went. They walked to their fields, they walked to their friends' houses, and they even walked to carry heavy things. But one day, someone in Mesopotamia had an idea. "What if we could make something that would help us carry things without having to walk so much?" they thought. And so they invented the wheel! The first wheels were made of wood and were used to make carts and wagons.

People could now carry heavy things like stones, grain, and even water much more easily. This invention changed everything!

Domesticating... crops?!

Before people started farming, they would hunt and gather food. But around 12,000 years ago, people figured out how to plant their own crops like wheat and barley. They learned how to cultivate the land and take care of the plants. This was a big change in the course of humanity as it allowed people to settle down in one place and build communities, rather than continuously travelling.

Shark!

A long, long time ago, there was a shark that was so big, it could swallow a car whole! This shark was called the Megalodon, and it lived around 2 million years ago. The Megalodon was the largest shark ever known, growing up to 60 feet long. That's longer than a school bus! The Megalodon had teeth that were as big as a person's hand, and it used them to eat whales, dolphins, and other big sea creatures. Luckily, the Megalodon is extinct now, so we don't have to worry about swimming with it.

Metalworks

People didn't have metal tools like we do today. They had to use stone tools, which were hard to make and not very strong. But then, around 6,000 years ago, someone had an idea. "What if we could melt metal and make it into tools?" they thought. And so they started experimenting with copper and bronze and eventually iron, which could be shaped when molten. They found that metal tools were much stronger and more durable than stone tools. Soon, people all over the world were making tools, swords, armor and jewelry.

Literacy

Before people were able to write, they would tell stories and pass down information orally. But around 5,000 years ago, the Sumerians in Mesopotamia figured out how to write things down. They used a system called cuneiform, which involved making marks on clay tablets with a stylus. The development of this writing system ended prehistory, and started a new era where historical events got documented in writing!

ANCIENT EGYPT

Ancient Egypt lasted for thousands of years and began around 5000 BC. They worshiped many gods and goddesses, built massive temples, and invented many things we still use today. They constructed pyramids and developed advanced medical knowledge. The New Kingdom was a time of great expansion and military conquest. The Egyptians believed in the afterlife and mummified their dead. Ancient Egypt civilization was centred around the River Nile and lasted for nearly 5000 years!

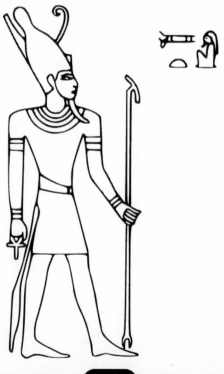

The Great Pyramid

Deep in the heart of ancient Egypt lies the Great Pyramid of Giza, a massive structure that towers over everything else in the area. It was built as a tomb for the pharaoh Khufu. It is one of the Seven Wonders of the Ancient World and is still standing today. The pyramid is made of over 2 million blocks of stone, each weighing around 2.5 tons. It was built by thousands of workers over a period of 20 years. and it was originally over 146 meters tall! Imagine building something like this in the middle of the desert with the technology they had back then!

Hieroglyphs

The Egyptians had a writing system called hieroglyphics. It was a form of writing that used pictures to represent words and sounds. The pictures were carved into stone or painted on papyrus scrolls. It was a very complicated writing system that only scribes, who were specially trained, could read and write. An example is shown, which is the name "Cleopatra" spelt in Egyptian hieroglyphics!

Gods & Goddesses

In ancient Egypt, people believed in many different gods and goddesses; over 2000 of them existed, each with their own specific role to play. There was Ra, the sun god; Osiris, the god of the afterlife, dead, life, fertility and agriculture; Isis, the goddess of magic and motherhood; Anubis, the god of the underworld and protector of graves and many others. Each god or goddess was associated with certain symbols, like a hawk or a crocodile, and they were often depicted in paintings and sculptures wearing elaborate clothing and jewelry.

Cleopatra

Cleopatra was a famous queen of Egypt, but did you know that she was actually Greek? As such, her native language was Greek and she had to learn Hieroglyphics before becoming queen, bringing the total number of languages she spoke to 9! She was the last pharaoh of Egypt, before Egypt became part of the Roman Empire. She had relationships with two of the most powerful men in the world at the time, Julius Caesar and Mark Antony.

Ancient Egyptians wore makeup

Both men and women in ancient Egypt wore makeup. They used a black eyeliner kohl to darken areas around their eyes, red ochre for their lips, and henna to dye their hair. They believed that makeup had magical properties and could protect them from evil spirits. They also believed that wearing makeup made them look more beautiful and gave them confidence.

Paper!

The ancient Egyptians were the first people to make paper. They used a plant called papyrus to make a type of paper. They would cut the papyrus into thin strips, lay them out in two layers, and then press them together. This created a strong, flat sheet of paper that they could write on.

Brush your teeth

Toothpaste was invented by the ancient Egyptians and was made from a mixture of crushed eggshells, myrrh, and pumice, a type of rock.

Ancient Egyptians love floods.

The Nile River was the lifeblood of ancient Egypt, since Egypt is situated in the super-hot Sahara Desert. It was a source of water, food, and transportation. Every year, the Nile would flood, depositing rich soil on the banks. This made the land very fertile, and allowed the ancient Egyptians to grow crops like wheat, barley, and flax. The Egyptians worshipped a god called Hapi, known as the god of floods.

Tutankhamun, the 9 year old Pharaoh

Tutankhamun became king when he was just 9 years old after he was next in line upon his father's death. Tutankhamun was too young to rule by himself, so he had advisors to help him make important decisions. Even though he was young, King Tut was an important and powerful leader in ancient Egypt. He became famous when the discovery of tomb in 1922 contained lots of treasure including a golden mask, giving us more information about Ancient Egypt.

Sphinx

Imagine you are walking through the desert in ancient Egypt, and you see a giant statue with the head of a person and the body of a lion. That's the Sphinx! The Sphinx is a famous statue that was built more than 4,500 years ago. It was built by the ancient Egyptians to guard a pyramid, which was the tomb of a Pharaoh. The Sphinx is over 240 feet long and 66 feet tall. It was a symbol of strength and power in ancient Egypt.

The Rosetta Stone

The Rosetta Stone is a big, black stone with writing on it in three different languages: Greek, Demotic, and hieroglyphics. It was found in 1799 in Egypt by a French soldier and it is called the Rosetta Stone because it was discovered in the town of Rosetta. The Rosetta Stone is important because it helped people learn how to read hieroglyphics and therefore uncover the secrets of ancient Egypt. The stone had the same message written in three different languages, so scholars were able to use the Greek script to translate the hieroglyphics. It's like having a secret code and finally finding the key to unlock it!

Are you a cat person?

Cats were very important in ancient Egypt. They were considered sacred animals and were worshipped as gods. People believed that cats had magical powers and could protect them from harm. They also believed that cats could bring good luck and fortune. Egyptians even mummified their cats and buried them with treasures so they would have the same fortune and protection in the afterlife!

Playtime wasn't so different

Just like kids today, ancient Egyptian children loved to play! They played with toys like dolls, balls, and board games. Some of their favorite board games were called senet and mehen. Senet, translated to the game of passing through, was a game of strategy that was played on a board with 30 squares. Mehen, also called the snake game was a game that was played with marbles on a spiral-shaped board.

The Afterlife

The ancient Egyptians believed that when someone died, their spirit would go on to live in another world called the afterlife. They thought that the afterlife was a place where people could live forever and be happy. They also believed that people needed certain things to live comfortably in the afterlife, just like they needed things in their everyday life. So, when someone died, the Egyptians would bury them with all the things they might need, like clothes, food, and even their favorite jewelry - which is why treasures of gold are often shown inside the pyramids of Ancient Egypt themed movies.

But it wasn't just about burying things with the person. The ancient Egyptians also believed that the dead needed guidance in the afterlife, so they would include a Book of the Dead in their tombs. This book was filled with spells and instructions that were meant to help guide the person through the underworld and into the afterlife. The Book of the Dead would also provide protection and help the person overcome any obstacles they might face.

ANCIENT GREECE

Ancient Greece was a civilization that existed over 2,000 years ago in the Mediterranean region. They believed in many gods and goddesses, built impressive structures, created the Olympic Games, and were famous for epic poems like the Iliad and Odyssey. Greek philosophy includes famous thinkers like Socrates and Aristotle. They loved to celebrate and have fun with many festivals throughout the year. Greek mythology includes famous heroes like Hercules and Perseus, and mythical creatures like Medusa.

Ancient Greece

Sparta

Sparta was a city-state in ancient Greece that was known for its tough and disciplined soldiers. The Spartans believed that being a soldier was the most important thing in life, and they trained their boys from a young age to be warriors.

When a boy was born in Sparta, he was examined by officials to make sure he was healthy. If he wasn't, he would be left to die. If he was healthy, he would be raised by his mother until he was seven years old, and then he would be sent to live in a barracks with other boys.

In the barracks, the boys were trained in fighting, wrestling, and running. They were given very little food and were expected to be tough and disciplined at all times. They slept on hard beds and were not allowed to wear shoes or warm clothing, even in winter. When they were 18 years old, the boys became soldiers and were sent to live in barracks with other soldiers. They spent most of their time training and preparing for war. The Spartans were feared throughout Greece because of their strength and discipline.

Greek Gods & Goddesses

The ancient Greeks believed in many gods and goddesses, and each one had their own special powers and responsibilities. For example, Zeus was the king of the gods, and he ruled over the sky and thunder. Apollo was the god of music and poetry, and he was known for his beautiful singing voice. Athena was the goddess of wisdom and war, and she was often depicted wearing a helmet and carrying a shield. Aphrodite was the goddess of love and beauty, and she was said to be the most beautiful of all the gods. The ancient Greeks believed that these gods and goddesses were real, and that they controlled the world around them. They would pray to them and make offerings in their temples to ask for their help and protection. The gods and goddesses were also the subject of many stories and myths, which the Greeks used to explain the world around them.

For example, one myth tells the story of how Zeus became the king of the gods. According to the myth, Zeus was born to the Titan Cronus and his wife Rhea. Cronus was afraid that one of his children would overthrow him, so he swallowed them all as soon as they were born. However, Rhea managed to save Zeus by hiding him on the island of Crete.

When Zeus grew up, he came back and challenged his father. With the help of his brothers and sisters, Zeus was able to defeat Cronus and become the king of the gods. The ancient Greeks believed that this myth explained why there were thunderstorms and earthquakes, and why Zeus was so powerful.

The First To Vote

In ancient Athens, the citizens had a say in how their city was run. They would gather in a large assembly to vote on laws and policies. This was called democracy, which means "rule by the people."

At the assembly, citizens would listen to speeches and then vote on issues. They used a system of colored stones to vote: a white stone meant "yes," a black stone meant "no," and a blank stone meant "abstain." The majority vote would win.

The Olympics

The first ever Olympics were held in 776BC, in Olympia in ancient Greece. Olympics were a huge event that everyone looked forward to. People from all over Greece would come to Olympia to watch athletes compete. The athletes were all men, and they trained for years to be able to compete in the games. They would light a flame to symbolize the start of the games. The athletes would then compete in events such as running and jumping over the next few days, and the winner would receive a wreath made of olive leaves.

The ancient Greeks believed that the Olympics were a way to honor the gods, and they dedicated the games to Zeus, the king of the gods. They believed that Zeus watched over the games and rewarded the athletes who performed the best.

Inventing The "Alphabet"

The English alphabet uses the letters from the Latin writing system, which in itself is derived from Greek. Therefore, the word "alphabet" comes from the first two letters of Greek - alpha and beta.

Great Minds Think Alike

A long time ago, in ancient Greece, there was a wise philosopher named Aristotle. A philosopher is someone who thinks and questions the world around them. He was very a smart man whose knowledge on math, science, and philosophy is still admired today. Many people wanted to learn from him, and one of those people was a young boy named Alexander, who would come to be known as Alexander the Great. Alexander The Great would go on to greatly expand his Empire, from a small one in Europe, to include most of the Middle East and even up to India.

Banned

The Greeks had a special way of voting called "ostracism," which involved writing the name of a person they wanted to banish from the city on a shard of pottery. If enough people wrote the same name, that person would have to leave the city for 10 years.

Bless You!

The ancient Greeks believed that a sneeze was a sign of good luck, and they would say "health" or "long life" when someone sneezed. They also believed that the soul could escape the body during a sneeze, so they would cover their mouths to prevent it from leaving.

Pythagoras

Another great mathematician and philosopher, Pythagoras was one day walking through a marketplace when he heard the sounds of hammers and saws. He followed the noise to a group of builders who were working on a roof. They were having trouble figuring out how long each side of the roof needed to be in order to make it strong and stable. Pythagoras stepped in to help the builders with a mathematical theory he had - and it worked! The triangular shaped roof was stable as the builders used Pythagoras' Theorem to calculate the diagonal length of a right-angled triangle. His formula is still used today and taught in many schools, so if you haven't yet heard about it, you will soon!

The Defeat Of Medusa

Medusa was a gorgon who had venomous snakes for hair and could turn people to stone just by looking at them. Many people were afraid of her and no one dared to approach her. However, a hero named Perseus was brave enough to try to defeat her. He went on a journey to find Medusa, and along the way, he met some helpful gods who gave him a special sword and shield. When he finally reached Medusa's lair, he used the shield to look at her reflection instead of looking directly at her. Then, he used the sword to chop off her head.

After defeating Medusa, Perseus used her head as a weapon against his enemies. He would pull it out of his bag and use it to turn his enemies to stone. Eventually, Perseus gave Medusa's head to Athena, a Greek Goddess and protector of cities, to place on her shield to help fulfil her duty. Athena, to this day, watches over one city more than the rest, and of course, that city is Athens, the current capital city of Greece.

ANCIENT ROME

Ancient Rome was a great civilization that lasted for over 1,000 years. They were famous for their engineering, art, military, and religion. They built amazing structures like the Colosseum and had a strong military that conquered vast areas of the western world. After a time of peace and prosperity called the Pax Romana that lasted for 200 years until 183 A.D., the empire began to decline and was eventually invaded by barbarian tribes. Despite this, the legacy of Ancient Rome continues to impact our world today!

Colosseum

The Colosseum in Rome is a huge amphitheater that was built over 2,000 years ago. It was used for all kinds of events, including animal shows and gladiator contests, where men would fight to the death with swords and shields for the entertainment of the crowds. The Colosseum could hold up to 80,000 people, which is more than most modern sports stadiums can hold! The richest people of the colosseum had seats closest to the action. Today, anyone can visit the colosseum in Rome, go inside and walk around the grounds!

A Country Formed By Two Brothers

According to legend, the city of Rome was founded by twin brothers named Romulus and Remus. They were abandoned as babies and raised by a she-wolf. When they grew up, they decided to build a city on the spot where the she-wolf had nursed them. However, they got into an argument over who would be the ruler of the city, and Romulus ended up killing Remus. This is how Rome got its name - from Romulus.

Ancient Rome

Humble Beginnings

Before the Roman Empire as you know existed, there was a country called the Roman Republic that had the same people, but was smaller in size, initially covering just a portion of the land Italy has today. Like Ancient Greece, they had a democratic system, and they had a strong army and built impressive things, such as roads and water supply for their people. They even developed a legal system. All this effort would help them grow and serve as a great help into the success in the Roman Empire.

The Roman Empire

The Roman Empire began when Augustus, who was married to Cleopatra was pronounced emperor. The empire lasted for a really long time – over 500 years, where was one of the most powerful empires in history, spreading across Europe, Africa, and the Middle East! However, eventually the empire became too big to control, and it started to fall apart. In 476 AD, the last emperor of Rome was overthrown by a Germanic leader called Odoacer, and the empire came to an end.

An Army Like No Other

The Roman army was famous for being well-trained and disciplined. They were equipped with some of the best weapons and armor of the time, and they were organized into groups called legions. The Roman army conquered a lot of territory, from Iraq to the United Kingdom, however, it wasn't just their weapons and tactics that made them so successful - it was also their ability to work together as a team.

10 Months

In ancient Rome, the calendar was a little different than the one we use today. Instead of having 12 months, they only had 10! The year started in March, which was the first month of the year. That means January and February didn't even exist yet!

July and August were named after two Romans: Julius Caesar and Augustus. Julius Caesar was a famous general who conquered a lot of territory for Rome, and Augustus was the first emperor of Rome. They were both so important that they got months named after them!

Ancient Rome

Bath Time

The Romans were famous for their public baths, which were like large swimming pools where people could bathe, socialize, and exercise. The Romans loved to take baths! They would go to public baths, which were like large swimming pools with different rooms for hot and cold water. People would bathe, socialize, and exercise at the baths. It was a great way for people to relax and stay healthy.

Missing Letters

The Roman alphabet had only 23 letters, and did not include the letters j, u or w.

Feed Me

Romans used to eat lying down on a couch while being fed by their servants. This was called a "triclinium" and was often done during dinner parties. Imagine lying down on a couch while someone fed you delicious food! In Ancient Rome, wealthy people would do just that. They would lie down on a special couch called a "triclinium" and be served food by their servants. This was a way for them to show off their wealth and status to their guests.

You Know More Latin Than You Think!

The ancient Romans spoke a language called Latin. It was the language of the government and the educated elite. Even though Latin is not spoken much anymore, it has had a big impact on many modern languages. For example, many English words come from Latin, like "exit" and "incredible", as well as many words used in medicine, science and law. French, Spanish, and Italian are all Romance languages that evolved from Latin, with Italian being one of the closest relatives of the language Romans used to speak!

Gods and Goddesses in Rome

The ancient Romans believed in many gods and goddesses. Their pantheon of gods was based on the Greek pantheon, which means they had many of the same gods and goddesses as the Greeks. However, the Romans gave the gods and goddesses different names and personalities. For example, Zeus in Greek mythology was known as Jupiter in Roman mythology, and Poseidon in Greek mythology was known as Neptune in Roman mythology. Most of the planets in our solar system would take their names from Roman mythology.

Romans Loved To Party!

The ancient Romans loved to celebrate! They had many festivals and holidays throughout the year. One of the most famous was Saturnalia, which was a winter solstice celebration. This festival lasted for a whole week and involved lots of feasting, gift-giving, and general merrymaking. People would exchange gifts and wear funny hats, and even the slaves were allowed to join in the celebrations! It was a time of joy and goodwill towards others.

A Different Kind Of Party

The festival of Lupercalia was a yearly celebration in Ancient Rome that took place on February 15th. During this festival, men would run around naked through the streets of Rome, wearing only a goat or dog skin around their waist. These men were called the Luperci, and they would run through the streets hitting women with the animal skins they were wearing.

It was believed that being hit by the skins would make the women more fertile and increase their chances of having children. Also known as dies Februatus, the festival is the basis for the name of the month of Febrauary!

Save your pee

The Romans used urine as a cleaning agent: The ancient Romans used urine as a cleaning agent for their clothes and even for their teeth! They believed that the ammonia in urine was an effective cleaning agent, and so they would collect it in pots and use it for washing.

A New Religion Is Born

The Romans played a very important role in the history of Christianity. At the time when Jesus Christ was alive, the Roman Empire ruled much of the western world, including Judea, the region where Jesus lived. Jesus was born into a Jewish family, and the Romans had a complicated relationship with the Jews. Jesus was ordered to be executed by crucifixion by Pontius Pilate, the Roman ruler of the area of Judea.

After Jesus was crucified, his followers continued to spread his message and teachings, which eventually grew into the religion of Christianity. At first, Christianity was a small and forbidden religion in the Roman Empire. The Romans did not like it because it challenged the authority of the emperor and the traditional Roman gods. However, over time, Christianity grew in popularity and many people in the Roman Empire started to convert. In 313 AD, the Roman emperor Constantine issued the Edict of Milan, which made Christianity legal in the Roman Empire. This was a turning point for Christianity, as it allowed the religion to grow and spread even more. The Catholic Church, which is the largest branch of Christianity today, was founded in Rome and many of its traditions and practices were influenced by Roman culture and society. Many cathedrals and churches worldwide were built with inspiration from Ancient Roman architecture.

Can I Have A Pay Raise?

Roman soldiers were paid in salt: The word "salary" comes from the Latin word "salarium," which was the payment that Roman soldiers received for their service. This payment was actually a ration of salt, which was a valuable commodity in ancient Rome.

IMPERIAL CHINA

Imperial China was a time period where emperors held great power and created impressive structures and inventions, including the Forbidden City, gunpowder, the compass, and porcelain. The Silk Road connected China to the rest of the world, and the imperial examination system helped to choose leaders. The Terracotta Army and dragons were also important parts of this time period.

Imperial China

The Terracotta Army

The Terracotta Army is an incredible discovery made in 1974 in China. It's a huge collection of clay soldiers that were buried with Emperor Qin Shi Huangdi, who was a powerful ruler of China over 2,000 years ago. The soldiers are as real people! There are thousands of them, and they're all unique with different hairstyles, expressions, and clothing. The Terracotta Army was created to protect the emperor in the afterlife, which is a belief that many people had during that time. It's like they thought that the emperor would still need soldiers to protect him even after he died.

I can see the sea

Imperial China is the period of China lasting from 223 BC to 1603 AD, a very long time. During this time, the Chinese land varied in size, but normally stretched from the Himalaya mountains to the Pacific Ocean, making it a huge country, about the size of the USA, and almost as big as Europe!

Son of Heaven

In ancient China, the emperor was one of the most important people in the entire country. The emperor was believed to have divine powers, which means that he was seen as someone who had special abilities and was almost like a god. The emperor was given a special title, "Son of Heaven," which showed just how important he was. This title meant that the emperor was seen as a link between heaven and earth. People believed that the emperor could communicate with the gods, and that he had the power to make things happen just by saying them out loud. The emperor was also responsible for making important decisions that affected the entire country. Because of all these special beliefs and powers, the emperor was someone who was deeply respected and admired by the people of China.

Ice Cream

The Chinese invented ice cream over 2,000 years ago, using a mixture of milk, rice, and snow!

Can I Have A Pet… Panda?!

Chinese emperors were some of the most powerful people in ancient China, and they had many interesting customs and beliefs. One of those beliefs was that pandas, which are cute and fluffy animals, could bring good luck and fortune. The emperors loved pandas so much that they even kept them as pets in their palaces. Pandas were considered special because they were rare, and they only lived in certain parts of China. The emperors would sometimes give pandas as gifts to foreign leaders to show how powerful and wealthy they were. Even today, pandas are still seen as symbols of good luck and fortune in China!

Have A Seat

Isn Imperial China, the emperor was the most powerful person in the entire country, and his throne was a symbol of that power. The throne was called the Dragon Throne because it was decorated with many different kinds of dragons, which were mythical creatures that were believed to be powerful and wise. The dragons on the throne were often made of gold, jade, or other precious materials, and they were carved in great detail to make them look as realistic as possible. The throne was also decorated with other important symbols, such as the phoenix, which was a bird that was also seen as a symbol of power and royalty. The Dragon Throne was located in the Forbidden City, which was the emperor's palace in Beijing, and it was only used for very special occasions.

Forbidden City

The Forbidden City in Beijing is one of the most famous landmarks in China. It's a massive palace that was built over 500 years ago and was the home of the Chinese emperors for many generations. The palace is called the "Forbidden City" because it was off-limits to regular people. Only the emperor, his family, and his closest advisors were allowed to enter. The palace was huge, with over 9,000 rooms, and it was beautifully decorated with colorful paint, intricate carvings, and gold leaf. The palace was also surrounded by a high wall and a moat, which helped to keep it safe from intruders. Over the centuries, the Forbidden City was the center of political and social life in China. Many important decisions were made there, and it was the site of many grand ceremonies and events. Today, the Forbidden City is open to the public, and it's a popular tourist destination where people can learn about the rich history and culture of China.

The Great Wall Of China

The Great Wall of China is one of the most famous landmarks in the world. It's a long wall that stretches across China, and it was built over 2,000 years ago. The wall was built to keep out invaders who might try to attack China from the north. The wall was not built by machines, but rather by soldiers and peasants who were conscripted by the emperor. This means that they were ordered to work on the wall, even if they didn't want to. It was a difficult and dangerous job, and many people died while working on the wall. The soldiers and peasants had to carry heavy bricks and stones up steep mountainsides, and they had to work in all kinds of weather. But despite the difficult conditions, they managed to build a wall that was over 13,000 miles long! Over the centuries, the wall was maintained and expanded by different emperors, and it became a symbol of China's strength and determination. Today, the Great Wall of China is one of the most popular tourist attractions in the world, and people from all over come to see this amazing feat

Gunpowder

The Chinese are known for many great inventions, including one that had a huge impact on warfare and celebrations around the world: gunpowder. Gunpowder is a mixture of chemicals that explodes when it's ignited, and it was invented by Chinese alchemists over a thousand years ago. At first, gunpowder was used mainly for fireworks displays, which were very popular in China. The Chinese loved to set off fireworks to celebrate special events, like weddings, births, and holidays. But later on, gunpowder was also used in warfare. The Chinese discovered that if they put gunpowder in a tube and ignited it, the tube would shoot out a small object at high speed. This was the beginning of the gun. The Chinese continued to improve the gun over the centuries, and eventually, it became one of the most important weapons in the world.

Imperial China

What is a dynasty?

Imperial China was ruled by a series of powerful families known as dynasties. These dynasties were like long-lasting kingdoms, with one family ruling over the entire country for many years at a time. There were many dynasties throughout China's long history, but some of the most famous ones were the Qin, Han, Tang, Song, and Ming dynasties.

Can You Past This Test?

In imperial China, the government officials were chosen through a system called the imperial examination system. This system was used to select the most talented and intelligent individuals to serve as government officials. The imperial examination system was based on the principles of Confucian philosophy, which emphasized the importance of education and knowledge. Confucianism taught that the most important duty of government officials was to serve the people with honesty and integrity, and the imperial examination system was designed to select officials who were capable of fulfilling this duty.

The Silk Road

The Silk Road was a very important trade route that has existed since ancient times. It was a network of roads, paths, and waterways that connected China with the Middle East and Europe. This route was called the "Silk Road" because one of the main things that was traded on the route was silk, which was produced in China and highly prized in other parts of the world. In Imperial China, silk was invented as a superior fabric for writing on and in clothing, and had great demand.

The Silk Road was not just for trading silk, though. Many other goods were traded along the route as well, including porcelain, spices, tea, porcelain, and precious stones. Porcelain is another invention from China that was in high demand, for use in plates - giving the name for high quality plates as fine China. The Silk Road also facilitated the exchange of ideas, cultures, and religions. Merchants and travelers who used the Silk Road brought new ideas and technologies to different parts of the world, and they also learned from the people they met along the way.

The Silk Road was a very long and dangerous

route, and travelers had to be very brave to make the journey. They had to cross mountains, deserts, and rivers, and they had to deal with bandits and other dangers. Despite these challenges, many people were willing to make the journey because they knew that the rewards could be great. The Silk Road helped to connect China with the rest of the world, and it played an important role in the development of trade, culture, and technology in ancient times. Today, the Silk Road is still remembered as an important part of China's history and cultural heritage.

Imperial Gardens

The gardens were often designed with special features that reflected the natural world, such as rocks, trees, waterfalls, and ponds. The landscape architects who designed the gardens were highly skilled, and they would spend years planning and constructing each garden to ensure that it was perfect. The gardens were also designed to be very peaceful and calming, with winding paths, small bridges, and hidden nooks and crannies where visitors could sit and reflect.

Mythology!

Chinese mythology is full of gods, goddesses, spirits, and legendary creatures that helped the Chinese understand the world around them, and their place in it.

These include the Jade Emperor, who was the ruler of heaven, and the Goddess of Mercy, who was known for her compassion and kindness.

In addition to gods and goddesses, Chinese mythology is also full of legendary creatures like dragons, which were believed to bring good luck and fortune, and the phoenix, which was a symbol of rebirth and renewal.

Inventions

Imperial China invented much more than we have talked about. The Chinese invented the abacus which is a device that makes it easy to count and do calculations. They realised that the Earth was magnetic and invented the compass which tells you which way is North and South. They were the first to invent a printing press to produce books in much larger quantities, nearly 1000 years before the western world. They even invented a seismometer which recorded the strength of an earthquake!

TP

The Chinese were one of the first civilizations to use toilet paper. It was invented in the 2nd century BC, and the Emperor himself was said to have ordered it to be made for him.

Monkey King

The legend of the Monkey King, also known as Sun Wukong, is an important part of Chinese mythology and has been a beloved story in Chinese culture for centuries.

According to the legend, the Monkey King was born from a stone egg on a mountain. He learned magic and martial arts from a Taoist master and became the king of the monkeys. He was known for his mischievous and sometimes rebellious nature, but he was also very intelligent and resourceful.

The Monkey King became involved in the battle between the gods and demons when he was invited to join the gods as a disciple. He proved himself to be a powerful ally, using his strength and magical abilities to help defeat the demons.

The Monkey King is known for his loyalty, bravery, and cleverness. He has become a symbol of rebellion and a hero to many in Chinese culture.

THE MAYANS, AZTECS & INCAS

The Mayans, Aztecs, and Incas were ancient civilizations in Central and South America. The Mayans existed in Central America the earliest, from around 2000BC and were an advanced society, known for their pyramids, such as those within Chichen Itza, and mythology. The Aztecs were known for their brutal human sacrifices, advanced agriculture, and impressive city planning, and fell to the Spanish in 1521. The Incas were the largest pre-Columbian empire in America, known for their road networks, quipus, and impressive ruins like Machu Picchu in present day Peru. The legacies of these civilizations are still present today and attract many tourists!

American Pyramids!

The Mayans were skilled builders and built pyramids which were typically used as temples or burial sites for important rulers. The most famous is the Pyramid of Kukulcan, located in the Mayan city of Chichen Itza. It is a huge pyramid that was built to honor the Mayan god Kukulcan. The pyramid has four sides, each with a staircase that has 91 steps. If you add up all the steps, including the top platform, there are 365 steps in total, which is the same as the number of days in a year!

For Religion

For the Mayans, Aztec and Icas, religion was a fundamental part of their daily lives. They believed in many gods and goddesses who controlled various aspects of the natural world, such as the sun, rain, and crops. To ensure that these gods and goddesses were pleased and that their needs were met, the Mayans practiced various rituals and ceremonies. One of the most controversial of these practices was human sacrifice, which involved offering a person's life to the gods in exchange for their favor. Human sacrifice was not practiced by all communities, but it was a significant part of some of their religious traditions. The victims were often prisoners of war, slaves, or even members of the community who were chosen for their physical or mental characteristics. They were treated with great respect and given food, drink, and other comforts before their sacrifice. There were several methods of human sacrifice used, including decapitation, heart removal, and drowning. The sacrificial act was often performed by a priest, who would wear special clothing and use special tools. The body of the victim was then often burned, and their ashes were either scattered or placed in a sacred urn.

Whats The Number Before One?

The Mayans first invented the concept of zero in mathematics, which was a big deal for doing complex maths. However, since Mayans had no contact with the Western world until much later, the Islamic Caliphates in the middle east is credited for giving the West the idea of using a zero in their numbers.

Competitive Sport

Mayans played a game called Pok-a-Tok that was a combination of soccer and basketball. The game was played on a ball court that was typically shaped like a capital I. The objective of the game was to hit a heavy rubber ball through a hoop using only the players' hips. The ball was made of solid rubber, which made it difficult to control and move around the court.

The game was often played during festivals and important events, and the ball court was a central gathering place for the community. The game was believed to have religious significance, and it was often played as a way to honor the gods.

There were several rules to the game of Pok-a-Tok. For example, players could not use their hands or feet to touch the ball, only their hips. Additionally, the ball could not be allowed to touch the ground during the game. If a player broke one of these rules, they would be punished, sometimes even with death! Playing Pok-a-Tok was a very physically demanding task, and players needed to be in excellent shape to compete. The game required a great deal of skill, strength, and agility, and it was played by both men and women. The Aztec had a similar game called ullamaliztli.

Hieroglyphic!

Just like Ancient Egypt, Mayans, and to some degree the Aztecs used their own hieroglyphs in their writing system. They were detailed images that often combined several different elements to represent a single word or concept. For example, a hieroglyph might depict a person, an animal, a plant, and a number all at once. These symbols were often carved into stone or written on bark paper using ink made from plant materials.

Chocolate Money

Mayans, Incas and Aztecs all used cocoa beans as their currency!

The Sun God

The Sun God was possibly the most important god because the sun god would give people light, warmth and allow crops to grow and farm animals to be fed. In the Aztec, Mayan and Inca civilizations, they believed that their sacrifices kept the sun turning through the sky. They monitored the sun with precise calendars and many of their structures are aligned with the sun and create various illusions when the sun is in a certain place in the sky.

Machu Picchu

Machu Picchu was built by the Inca Empire in the 15th century on a steep mountain ridge. It is also called the Lost City Of The Incas as unlike most other Inca settlements, Machu Picchu was only discovered recently, making it one of the only existing Inca settlements remaining. Today, Machu Picchu is a popular tourist destination.

Languages

The original language spoken by the Inca is known as Quechua, and that language is still spoken by millions of people in South America today. Similar for the Mayan language, millions of people around central america can speak it today!

Sacred Animals

Ever need to get along with an Aztec? Just remember that they regard the jaguar as a sacred animal, and the owl as a sign of death and bad luck.

THE ISLAMIC GOLDEN AGE

The Islamic Golden Age was a time of great progress and innovation in Islamic civilization that lasted from the 8th to the 13th century. Muslims made important inventions and discoveries, as you will see. This period also saw the construction of beautiful mosques and palaces. The Islamic Golden Age was fueled by a culture of intellectual curiosity and it has shaped the culture of the Middle East today, as well as contributing greatly to the Western world.

Do you like calculus?

Up until the 9th century you could work out how to split 10 gold coins between people by just dividing 10 by the number of people. But imagine splitting an amount of gold coins by 4 people, with one receiving twice as many as the other 3. This would have been hard to solve until the invention of algebra by Al-Khwarizmi, whose invention has helped mathematicians solve complex equations easier. Of course, if you haven't heard of algebra yet, you will likely to alot in your math classes over the coming years! Good luck!

Inventing A Number

Using roman numerals was annoying when it came to doing math related things since there was no zero. The Arabic numerals, which used the 0-9 system, and had the number zero revolutionized the way people did math and counted, and so was introduced into western culture. So in a way, the number zero was invented by the Arabic people.

Story Time

During the Islamic Golden Age, people loved to be entertained, just like we do today. One of the most popular forms of entertainment was storytelling and one of the most famous collections of stories was called "One Thousand and One Nights," also known as "The Arabian Nights."

The stories in "One Thousand and One Nights" were originally told by storytellers from all over the Muslim world. The stories were often set in exotic locations, and they featured all kinds of characters, from sultans and princesses to merchants and thieves.

You may have heard of some stories from One Thousand and One Nights, such as Aladdin, Ali Baba and the Forty Thieves, and Sinbad the Sailor. These stories are still popular today, and they've been adapted into movies, TV shows, and even Disney cartoons!

In these stories, you'll find magic lamps, flying carpets, and hidden treasure. You'll also find brave heroes who use their wits and bravery to overcome evil villains. The stories are full of adventure and excitement!

The Islamic Golden Age

A new religion and a new empire

Islam was born in Mecca, in the region of Arabia in the 7th century and quickly spread, side-by-side with the birth of the Islamic empire, known as a caliphate. After the death of prophet Muhammad, the founder of Islam, successors known as Caliphs expanded their caliphates, and with it, Islam. The Islamic Golden Age saw three major caliphates, with great military strength taking the second caliphate to its greatest reaches. During this caliphate, known as the Umayyad caliphate, the size was enormous! The caliphate extended from Spain and Portugal to India, making it almost comparable to the size of the Roman Empire, and actually taking up alot of territory that used to belong to the Romans. The caliphate bought art and culture, with Islamic architecture prevalent on mosques and other buildings that can still be seen today. The caliphate struggled under invasion from the growing Mongol Empire, and by 1261, their capital city of Baghdad fell, and so with it the Islamic Golden Age.

THE VIKINGS

The Viking Age lasted from the late 8th century to the mid-11th century. The Vikings, known for their fighting skills and love of adventure, raided and traded in other countries, including the British Isles and North America. They were also skilled craftsmen and formed their own kingdoms. The Viking Age came to an end as they focused on building their own kingdoms and faced pressure from other groups. Despite its violent beginnings, the Viking Age was a time of exploration and adventure that left a lasting impact on the world.

Helmets With Horns

... don't exist. The image of a Viking wearing a helmet with horns has become iconic, but it is not accurate. Vikings did wear helmets, but they did not have horns. In fact, a helmet with horns would have been impractical in battle, as it would have made it easier for an opponent to knock the helmet off.

Runes

Runes were a set of symbols used by the Vikings to write messages and communicate with each other. Each symbol had a specific meaning, and they were often carved into wood or stone. Runes were not just used for writing messages; they were also believed to have magical properties. Each rune had its own special meaning, and some people believed that they could use them to cast spells or gain protection in battle. Today, runes are still used by some people who practice certain religions or spiritual beliefs. They are seen as a way to connect with the ancient past and to tap into their power and symbolism.

Pirate Raid

The word "Viking" comes from the Old Norse word "vikingr", which means "pirate raid". This reflects the Vikings' reputation as fierce raiders who would attack other lands and towns.

The Viking War Ship

Viking longboats were large, sturdy ships that the Vikings used to travel across the seas. They were designed for speed and maneuverability, and they were able to travel long distances quickly.

The longboats were made of wood, and they had a long, narrow shape with a pointed bow and stern. They were powered by oars and sails, and they were able to travel in shallow waters and even up rivers.

One of the most famous features of the Viking longboats was their dragon-head prow, which was a carving of a dragon's head at the front of the ship. This was believed to be a symbol of the Viking's strength and power, and it was also used to intimidate their enemies.

Inside the longboats, there was a large open area where the Vikings would sit and row the boat. They would also sleep and eat in this area during long journeys. The longboats were able to carry many people and supplies, which allowed the Vikings to travel far and wide and to raid other lands.

Equality

Viking women had more freedom than women in many other societies at the time. They could own property, make important decisions, and even divorce their husbands if they chose to do so.

Viking Gods

The Vikings had many gods and goddesses that they believed in and worshiped. These gods and goddesses were seen as powerful beings who could control the forces of nature and influence the lives of humans.

One of the most well-known Viking gods was Thor, the god of thunder and lightning. He was known for his mighty hammer and his ability to control the storms. The Vikings believed that by praying to Thor, they could protect themselves from danger and bring good luck.

Another important Viking god was Odin, the god of wisdom, war, and death. Odin was seen as the leader of the gods and was often depicted with one eye. The Vikings believed that by praying to Odin, they could gain wisdom and courage in battle.

Loki was another important Viking god, although he was often seen as a trickster who caused trouble for the other gods. He was known for his shape-shifting abilities and was often depicted as a mischievous figure.

There were many other Viking gods and goddesses, each with their own unique powers and personalities. For example, Freya was the goddess of love and fertility, while Tyr was the god of war and justice.

The Vikings believed that by honoring and worshiping these gods, they could gain their favor and protection. They would often make sacrifices and offerings to the gods, such as animals, food, or precious objects.

Valhalla

According to Viking mythology, Valhalla was a great hall in Asgard, the home of the gods. It was ruled by the god Odin, who was the chief of the Norse gods and the god of war, wisdom, and poetry. Odin was also known as the god of the dead, and he was said to have a keen interest in warriors who died in battle.

The Vikings believed that if they died in battle, they would be chosen by Odin to enter Valhalla. There, they would be greeted by the Valkyries, female warriors who served Odin and chose the bravest and strongest warriors to bring to Valhalla. The warriors who made it to Valhalla would be rewarded with a feast and would be allowed to fight each other to their heart's content.

In Valhalla, the warriors would fight each other with swords and other weapons, but they could not be killed or permanently injured. They would spend their days fighting and their nights feasting, drinking mead, and telling stories of their great deeds on Earth. The Vikings believed that this cycle would continue forever, and that they would be eternally honored in Valhalla. The belief in Valhalla was a central part of Viking culture and played an important role in motivating Viking warriors to fight bravely and fearlessly.

Barber? No thanks.

Vikings believed that having long hair and beards made them look more powerful and intimidating. They would often decorate their hair with beads or other ornaments, making it look even more impressive.

The Blacksmith

Blacksmithing was a very important trade during the Viking Age. Blacksmiths were skilled craftsmen who worked with metal, such as iron and bronze, to make a variety of items that the Vikings needed for everyday life. They worked individually in their own workshops, or shared a workshop with other blacksmiths.

The blacksmiths would use a forge, which is a type of oven, to heat the metal until it was red-hot. Then, they would use hammers and other tools to shape the metal into the desired shape. They would often make weapons, such as swords, axes, and spears, as well as tools, such as knives, farming equipment, and horseshoes.

The blacksmiths were highly respected in Viking society because they provided the Vikings with the weapons and tools they needed for survival. They were also often called upon to make jewelry and other decorative items.

Blacksmiths were usually men, but could also be women!

A Ballad For Ye

The Vikings loved to tell stories! They
would gather together around a fire or in a
hall and share stories of their adventures,
battles, and mythical creatures. These
stories were passed down from generation to
generation through oral tradition, which
means they were told out loud instead of
being written down.

Sometimes, the stories were set to music and
sung. These songs were called ballads, and
they were a way for the Vikings to remember
important events and share their culture
with others. The ballads were often sung in
a style that is called "skaldic," which
involves using metaphors and wordplay to
tell a story.

The Vikings believed that storytelling was
important because it helped to preserve
their history and culture. They also
believed that by sharing their stories, they
could inspire others and teach important
lessons.

Flat Earther

The Vikings believed that the world was flat,
and that it was surrounded by a great sea
that monsters lived in. They also believed
that the stars and constellations were gods
and goddesses.

Lief Erikson

Leif Erikson was a famous Viking explorer who is best known for being the first European to reach North America, about 500 years before Christopher Columbus. Leif Erikson was born in Iceland in the late 10th century, and he grew up in a family of explorers and traders.

As a young man, Leif Erikson sailed to Norway and became friends with King Olaf Tryggvason. The king converted Leif to Christianity, and Leif returned to Iceland to spread the religion among the Vikings.

In the year 1000 AD, Leif Erikson set sail from Greenland on a mission to explore lands to the west. He eventually reached the coast of what is now Canada, which he called Vinland. Leif Erikson and his crew spent a winter in Vinland, where they built a settlement and traded with the local Native Americans. They eventually returned to Greenland, where Leif's brother, Thorvald, set out to continue exploring Vinland.

Leif Erikson is remembered as a brave explorer who helped to open up new lands and opportunities for the Vikings. Today, he is celebrated as a national hero in Iceland, and his story has inspired many people to explore and discover new things.

Raid!

During the Viking Age, the Vikings raided towns, villages and monasteries all across Europe, and even as far as the Middle East. When the Vikings arrived at a place they wanted to raid, they would first scout the area to look for weaknesses in the defenses. They would then quickly launch an attack, using weapons like swords, axes, and spears to fight the people defending the town or village. The Vikings were skilled warriors, and their weapons were often sharper and more effective than those of their opponents.

The Vikings would then take anything valuable that they could find, such as gold, silver, and jewels. They would also take livestock and people as slaves to sell or keep as servants. After they had taken what they wanted, they would usually set fire to the town or village and sail away with their loot.

Viking raids were a feared and destructive part of Viking culture, and they caused a lot of damage to the places they attacked. However, the Vikings also used their raiding skills to become successful traders and establish trade networks across Europe and beyond.

Not Just Raiders

The Vikings were not just raiders; they were also skilled traders who would travel to other lands to trade goods. They would trade items such as furs, weapons, and jewelry for other goods. Viking were also skilled farmers. They grew crops such as barley and rye, and they raised animals like cows, pigs, and sheep. Their favorite drink was mead, an alcoholic drink made from fermented honey and water.

Not Just Raiders

Vikings were very clean people and would often bathe at least once a week, which was much more than other people in Europe at the time. They also had a tool called a "comb-scraper" which they used to keep clean.

An End Of An Era

The Viking Age came to an end after Christianity spread into Norse culture and began shaping society. The Vikings began to focus on building their own kingdoms, such as the newly formed kingdoms of Denmark, Norway and Sweden. They also settled in areas such as England, Scotland, and Ireland, and they formed their own governments and cultures.

THE CRUSADES

The Crusades were a series of wars between Christians from Europe and Muslims from the Middle East over control of the holy city of Jerusalem. Remember how during The Islamic Golden Age, the caliphate captured most of the land from the Christian Roman Empire, including areas seen as holy by both religions.

The first Crusade was the most famous, and although the Christians managed to capture Jerusalem, the Muslims eventually regained control. Many more Crusades followed, but the Christians were never able to fully conquer the region.

The Crusades

Upgrade

During the Crusades, both the Christian and Muslim armies had to develop new weapons and tactics to gain an advantage over their enemy. The constant fighting led to new ideas and inventions that changed the way wars were fought.

One of the most important weapons that was developed during the Crusades was the crossbow. A crossbow is a type of bow that is mounted on a stock, which makes it easier to aim and fire. It was a very powerful weapon and could pierce armor, making it very effective in battles.

For Religion!

During the Crusades, many traveled months by sea just to reach the Holy Land in the modern-day Middle East. Most were doing it because they believed God wanted them to, and some Crusaders even believed that if they died while fighting for Christianity, they would go straight to heaven, similar to the Viking belief in Valhalla. This belief led to some Crusaders deliberately seeking out dangerous situations in battle.

The Crusades

Richard The Lionheart

Richard the Lionheart was a king of England who was a hero of the Crusades. He was known for his bravery and courage, his skills as a warrior, and his determination to defend the Christian faith.

Richard was a very tall and strong man, so strong that its been said that he is able to bend an iron bar with his bare hands. He fought in many battles during the Crusades, including the Battle of Arsuf, which was a major victory for the Christian army.

Despite his reputation as a warrior, Richard was also known for his kindness and his generosity. He was a knight who lived by a strict code of honor, and he was respected by both his friends and his enemies.

Robin Hood

Robin Hood is a legendary hero who is known for his bravery and his skill with a bow and arrow. He is said to have lived in England during the time of the Crusades, and he was known for stealing from the rich and giving to the poor. The legend of Robin Hood is said to have been inspired by the stories of the Crusaders who fought in the Holy Land.

The Crusades

The Knight's Code

During the Crusades, the Crusaders had to communicate with each other in order to plan their battles and carry out their missions. However, they couldn't risk their enemies intercepting their messages, so they developed their own secret code language called "the Knights' Code".

The Knights' Code was a set of secret words and phrases that only the Crusaders knew the meaning of. They would use this code to communicate with each other during battles and on secret missions without their enemies being able to understand what they were saying.

For example, instead of saying "attack the castle at dawn", they might say something like "the rooster crows at dawn" to convey the same message. This way, even if their enemies heard their messages, they wouldn't be able to understand what was being said. The Knights' Code was a very important tool for the Crusaders, as it helped them to keep their plans and strategies secret!

A Sticky Situation

The Holy Land in the modern-day Israel and Palestine is so holy because it forms the setting for most of the biblical events, such as the Birth of Jesus. However, it is not just holy for Christians, but for Jews (they too believe in Jesus and God) and also for Muslims (they also believe in Jesus and God). You can begin to see why this area has so much conflict! Originally, the Holy Land belonged to the Christian Roman Empire, but as the empire fell, it was made part of the Islamic Caliphates during the Islamic Golden Age. The mostly Christian Europe were not too happy, and the Crusades formed their attempt to claim back the Holy Land, which was ultimately unsuccessful. As a result, inhabitants of the Holy Land today are mostly Jews and Muslims.

Reconquista

The Crusades didn't just happen in the Holy Land. Spain, once part of the Islamic Umayyad Caliphate also experienced it's own Crusades called Reconquista, where Christian Kingdoms in Northern Spain fought to claim back the rest of Spain from the caliphate, which was successful.

FEUDAL JAPAN

Feudal Japan was a period in Japanese history when the country was divided into small kingdoms, each ruled by a warlord called a daimyo. The era was characterized by fierce battles for power and control among the daimyos. Feudal Japan was also known for its unique culture, including tea ceremonies, cherry blossom season, and geisha fashion.

The Way Of The Samurai

Samurai were a special group of warriors in feudal Japan who worked for powerful leaders called daimyos. They were trained from a young age to be skilled in many different types of fighting, including sword-fighting and archery. They were taught how to use different types of swords, such as the long katana and the shorter wakizashi. Samurai were also trained in the art of horseback riding, which was important for travel and battle.

Samurai lived according to a strict code of honor called bushido, which emphasized loyalty, courage, and honor. They were expected to be brave in battle and to protect their lord at all costs. If a samurai failed to uphold their honor, they would be expected to commit seppuku, which was a ritual suicide performed by cutting one's own stomach with a short sword.

Despite the strict code of honor, not all samurai were perfect. Some samurai were known for their cruelty, while others were celebrated for their bravery and chivalry. However, all samurai were skilled warriors who played an important role in the history and culture of feudal Japan.

The Samurai's Outfit

Samurai were not only skilled warriors, but they also had a unique and distinctive outfit that they wore called a hakama. The hakama consisted of a pleated skirt that was worn over a pair of wide pants. The pants were usually made of silk or cotton and were tied around the waist with a thick belt called an obi.

The hakama was not only a practical outfit for samurai, but it was also a symbol of their status and honor. Samurai wore the hakama during important ceremonies and events, such as weddings, funerals, and battles. The color and design of the hakama would often indicate the rank and status of the samurai. For example, lower-ranking samurai would wear a plain or dark-colored hakama, while higher-ranking samurai would wear a more elaborate and colorful hakama.

Bushido

Samurai were expected to live according to the bushido code, which emphasized three things: complete loyalty, courage and fearlessness in battle, and honor in acting with honesty and integrity at all times.

A Legendary Samurai

Miyamoto Musashi was a legendary samurai in feudal Japan who was known for his exceptional sword-fighting skills. He was born in 1584 and started training in the art of swordsmanship at a young age. He quickly became known as one of the greatest swordsmen of his time.

Throughout his life, Miyamoto Musashi is said to have fought over 60 duels against other skilled swordsmen. He never lost a single duel and was known for his incredible speed, strength, and accuracy with a sword. Musashi developed his own unique style of sword-fighting, which he called Niten Ichi-ryu, or "two swords as one."

Despite his reputation as a fierce warrior, Musashi was also known for his wisdom and philosophy. He wrote a famous book called "The Book of Five Rings," which is still studied by martial artists and business leaders today. The book contains Musashi's teachings on strategy, tactics, and philosophy, and emphasizes the importance of mental preparation and focus in addition to physical training.

Ninja

The ninja were a special group of warriors in feudal Japan who were known for their unique skills in stealth and espionage. Unlike the samurai who served daimyos, the ninja worked for themselves or for clients who paid them for their services.

Ninja were highly skilled in a variety of techniques that allowed them to move quickly and quietly, hide in shadows, and blend in with their surroundings. They were trained in the art of disguise and could easily change their appearance to look like someone else. They also had extensive knowledge of poisons and could use them to incapacitate or kill their enemies.

The ninja's weapons and tools were extensive, as you will see soon, and it was the ninja's job to choose the right ones for the task. They also had a special tool called a grappling hook that allowed them to climb walls and buildings quickly and quietly.

The ninja's skills were highly valued in feudal Japan, especially during times of war when espionage and sabotage were important tactics. The ninja were hired to gather information, sabotage enemy fortifications, and even assassinate key targets.

A Ninja's Arsenal

One of the most famous ninja weapons was the shuriken, or throwing stars. These small, flat, sharp stars could be thrown with great accuracy and could cause serious injury to an opponent. Ninjas would often carry shuriken with them on missions, and they would use them to incapacitate or distract guards or enemies.

Another weapon commonly used by ninjas was the kusarigama. This was a combination of a sickle and a chain, and it was a versatile weapon that could be used for both close-range and long-range attacks. The sickle could be used to slash at an opponent, while the chain could be used to entangle them or to strike from a distance.

Ninjas also used a variety of other weapons, such as swords, knives, and spears, as well as tools such as grappling hooks and smoke bombs.

The Real Ones In Power

In feudal Japan, the emperor was the highest-ranking official and was considered the spiritual leader of the country, however, the emperor had very little real power over the government and the people. In reality, the true power in Japan was held by the shogun, who was the military leader of the country. The shogun held the real authority, and it was he who made the important decisions about the country's governance and defense.

The emperor was still an important figure in Japanese society, however. He was considered the symbol of Japan and the link to its rich history and traditions. Many Japanese people felt a deep reverence and respect for the emperor, and he played an important role in ceremonies and rituals that were central to Japanese culture.

Bonsai Tree

The Japanese art of "bonsai," which involves growing miniature trees in containers, originated during Feudal Japan as a way to bring nature inside the homes of wealthy aristocrats.

Sumo Wrestling

Sumo wrestling is a popular and traditional sport in Japan that has been around for hundreds of years. It involves two wrestlers, or rikishi, trying to push each other out of a circular ring, or dohyo, using various techniques and maneuvers.

The roots of sumo wrestling can be traced back to the feudal era in Japan, when samurai warriors would compete in wrestling matches as a way to hone their strength and combat skills. Over time, these matches evolved into a more formalized sport, with rules and regulations that governed the matches and determined the winner.

Today, sumo wrestling is a highly respected sport in Japan, with a professional league and many fans and followers. Wrestlers undergo rigorous training and practice for years to reach the highest levels of the sport.

Write Me A Poem

The haiku was born in Feudal Japan, a poem that consists of just 17 syllables. An example of one about Japan:

Mountains rise so high,
Cherry blossoms in the breeze,
Japan's beauty thrives.

Zen

Zen Buddhism is a type of Buddhism that originated in China and was introduced to Japan during the feudal era. Zen buddhism emphasizes the importance of meditation and mindfulness, and encourages people to focus on living in the present moment rather than dwelling on the past or worrying about the future.

Zen Buddhism was practiced by samurai in particular, who were drawn to its emphasis on self-discipline, mental focus, and personal enlightenment. Zen meditation was used as a way to improve their martial arts skills and prepare for battle, while others turned to Zen as a way to find inner peace and tranquility.

Over time, Zen Buddhism became an important part of Japanese culture. Zen gardens, for example, are a common feature in Japanese temples and homes, and are designed to promote relaxation and contemplation.

Kappa

People believed in many mythical creatures that they believed lived in the world around them. One of the most famous of these creatures was the "kappa," a mischievous water sprite that was said to live in rivers, ponds, and other bodies of water. According to legend, the kappa had a distinctive appearance, with greenish skin, webbed feet and hands, and a bowl-shaped depression on the top of its head that was filled with water. The kappa was known for its mischievous behavior, and was said to enjoy playing pranks on humans, such as pulling their hair or stealing their food.

In some stories, the kappa was also said to be a dangerous creature that would attack humans, especially children. Parents would warn their children not to go near bodies of water alone, for fear that they might encounter a kappa and be dragged under the water.

Despite its fearsome reputation, the kappa was also a popular subject of Japanese folklore and art. Many Japanese stories and poems feature kappa characters, and the creature has even made appearances in modern popular culture, such as in video games and anime.

THE BLACK DEATH

The Black Death was a deadly disease that spread across Europe in the 14th century, killing hundreds of millions of people. It was caused by a bacteria carried by fleas on rats, and was bought over to Europe from Asia in 1347, first arriving in Venice in Italy. Symptoms included a bad fever, vomiting, and painful swellings across the body called buboes. The disease had a devastating impact, killing over 75 million people, but also made some positive changes to society such as better pay for workers.

The Black Death

Why Was It Called The Black Death?

When someone caught the Black Death, they
would often start to feel very sick with a
high fever and vomiting. Then, painful
swellings called buboes would appear on
their body. These buboes were filled with
pus and were often very large and painful.
As the disease progressed, dark patches
would begin to appear on the skin of the
victim. These patches were a sign that the
disease was spreading and getting worse.
They would start out as small red spots and
then turn black as the skin died. The
combination of these black patches and the
painful buboes led to the disease being
called the "Black Death." It was a scary and
terrible disease, and people were very
afraid of catching it because there was no
known cure at the time.
The disease is also known as the bubonic
plague, and today thankfully, is curable.
Phew!

Try This Remedy

During the time of the Black Death, doctors
didn't know much about how diseases worked
or how to cure them. So, when people started
getting sick with the Black Death, they

tried all sorts of strange remedies to try to help them feel better. Some people would drink their own urine, which is something we know today is not helpful in fighting off diseases. Others believed that putting a live chicken on the buboes of the victim would draw out the disease. These remedies seem very weird and silly to us today, but people didn't know any better at the time. The truth is that there was no known cure for the Black Death, and people had to rely on their own immune systems to fight off the disease.

Preventing The Cause

As well as not knowing the cure, people didn't know what was causing the disease to spread. They thought it might be caused by evil spirits or the wrath of God. Cats were often associated with witchcraft and evil, so many people believed that cats were somehow responsible for the spread of the disease. Because of this, many cats were killed in an attempt to stop the disease from spreading. However, this actually made the problem worse. Cats are natural predators of rats, which are the real culprits that carried the fleas that spread the disease. With fewer cats around, there were more rats, and more fleas spreading the disease. It's a good lesson for us today – sometimes our fears and superstitions can lead us to do things that actually make problems worse instead of better.

Contagion

The Black Death was an extremely contagious disease, meaning it could easily spread from person to person. If someone was infected with the disease and coughed or sneezed, tiny droplets could be released into the air. These droplets contained the bacteria that caused the disease, and if someone else breathed them in, they could also become infected. The disease was so contagious that even being in the same room as someone who was infected could lead to getting the disease. This is why people were so scared of the Black Death, and why it spread so quickly.

The Worst Disease

All in all, between 30% and 60% of the population of Europe was wiped out and it would take over 150 years before the European population would recover.

The Black Death

Doctor, Doctor!

During the time of the Black Death, there were doctors who were called "plague doctors." These doctors wore very distinctive clothing to protect themselves from the disease. Plague doctors wore long robes that went all the way down to their feet. The robes were made of a special fabric that was treated with a chemical to help keep germs away. The doctors also wore a mask that covered their entire face. The mask had a long beak-like nose, which was filled with sweet-smelling herbs. The doctors believed that the sweet smell would help protect them from the bad smells of the disease, which they thought could make them sick. Plague doctors also carried a long stick that they would use to examine their patients without getting too close to them. Plague doctors would often give their patients medicines made from herbs, which they believed would help the body fight off the disease. They also used leeches to draw blood from their patients, which they thought would help balance the body's humors and make the patient feel better. Additionally, they would sometimes use special tools to try to drain the pus from the buboes that appeared on the patient's body. Although these treatments were not effective in curing the disease, the plague doctors were doing their best to help their patients in any way they could.

The Silver Lining

Although the Black Death was a horrible time, the Black Death taught society about the importance of hygiene measures not known before, such as washing hands, and so public cleanliness improved. The Black Death created a shortage of workers, and so each worker could demand more pay. This helped end the quite unfair system of feudalism, a system where peasant had to work just to have the right to own a place to live.

THE TUDORS

The Tudor era was a time in England's history that lasted from 1485 to 1603. It began with King Henry VII's victory in the battle of York, and covered some interesting characters, such as King Henry VIII who had six wives and created a new church called the Church of England, and Mary, who was nicknamed Bloody Mary and we shall see why in a bit. William Shakespeare was also born in this era, as well as famous explorers Francis Drake and Sir Walter Raleigh.

Witchcraft

Henry VIII, the king of England a long time ago, had 6 wives. His second wife, Anne Boleyn was accused of doing bad things. They said she was not faithful to Henry VIII and had a boyfriend who was not her husband. People also said she was a witch, which means she could do magic and use it to hurt others. These things made Henry VIII very angry, and he decided to have her killed. So, they took Anne Boleyn to a place called the Tower of London, and they cut off her head with a sword.

A Feast Fit For A King

One thing King Henry VIII was famous for was his love of food! Henry VIII loved to eat, and he liked to have really big meals with lots of different dishes. Reportedly, he would consume around 5000 calories a day, twice the recommended average for a grown man. One time, he had a feast where there were over 50 different courses! That means there were 50 different types of food that were served during the meal. Can you imagine how long that would take to eat?

The Tudors

Unhappy Parents

Henry VIII was a king of England a long time ago, and he was also a very religious man. He believed that it was very important to follow the rules of the church and to be a good Christian. Henry VIII was married to a woman named Catherine of Aragon, but they had some problems in their marriage. They didn't have any sons, and Henry VIII wanted a son to be his heir and take over the throne when he died. So, Henry VIII asked the Pope, who was the leader of the Catholic Church, for permission to divorce Catherine so he could marry someone else and have a son. But the Pope said no, because he believed that marriage was supposed to be forever, according to the wedding vows and could not be undone. This made Henry VIII very upset, and he decided to do something about it. He broke away from the Catholic Church to start his own church. This church became known as the Church of England, and it allowed Henry VIII to divorce Catherine and marry someone else. This was a big event in history and changed the way that religion was practiced in England.

Astrology

The Tudors were very interested in astrology, which is the study of how the position of the stars and planets can affect people's lives. They believed that certain times and dates were lucky or unlucky, depending on the position of the stars and planets. This belief in astrology was so strong that many royal documents, such as proclamations and treaties, were signed at specific times and dates that were considered to be lucky.

Tudor Sport

Henry VIII was very interested in sports. One sport he particularly enjoyed was jousting. Jousting was a type of competition where two knights rode horses and charged towards each other with long sticks called lances. The goal was to try to knock the other knight off his horse. Henry VIII was very good at jousting and would often compete in tournaments. He even had a special suit of armor made just for jousting. However, jousting was a dangerous sport, and Henry VIII suffered several injuries while competing, including one that nearly killed him. Despite the risks, Henry VIII continued to enjoy and participate in jousting throughout his life. Jousting was a popular sport in medieval times, and it was one of many ways that knights could demonstrate their skills and bravery.

Bloody Mary

Mary Tudor, also known as Bloody Mary by her opponents, was a queen who succeeded King Henry VIII's only son, Edward VI. Edward VI was only 15 when he died, and initially in his will left the crown for Jane. However Mary, daughter of King Henry VIII and his first wife, Catherine of Aragon, soon took over the crown after getting popular support and had Jane executed. Mary was a very religious person and believed strongly in the Catholic faith, a branch of Christianity that was common before Henry VIII's reforms. Therefore, when Mary became queen, she tried to return England to Catholicism after it had become Protestant. She even earned the nickname "Bloody Mary" because she executed a total of 283 notable Protestants by burning them on a wooden pole, while still alive. Queen Mary ruled for just 5 years before dying due to bad health.

The Tudors

Superstition

The Tudors had many unusual superstitions that they respected. They believed the number 9 was lucky, and so incorporated it into many design elements. They believed carrying a rabbit's foot was lucky, and so many people carried one at all times. They believed the color green was unlucky, so did not wear much green clothing, and they believed the sound of a bell could scare away evil spirits.

Stylish Houses

During the Tudor era, people didn't have the same kinds of building materials that we have today, such as bricks and concrete. Instead, Tudor Era houses were made of timber and wattle and daub. This means that the house had a wooden frame, which was filled in with a mixture of mud and straw. Tudor houses were often designed with steeply pitched roofs and large chimneys. The roofs were made of thatch, which is a type of dried grass, and the chimneys were made of stone. Tudor houses also had small, diamond-shaped windows with leaded glass. Many Tudor houses still stand today and are noticeable for their black or brown beams with white walls. Some people even live in Tudor houses today, where they can be seen in English cities such as Warwick, York and London. Unfortunately, the flammability of the materials of these houses contributed to the severity of the Great Fire Of London in 1666.

The Virgin Queen

After the death of Mary I, Queen Elizabeth I ruled for 45 years. She was only two years old when her mother, Anne Boleyn had her head cut off by her father, Henry VIII. Because of this, she could only become queen if her older half-siblings, Edward and Mary were no longer about and upon Mary's death, it was Elizabeth's time to shine.

She reversed much of what Mary I had done in trying to convert England back to Catholicism. She oversaw the flourishing of arts and culture such as Shakespeare, as well as explorers such as Francis Drake to new lands, which will be the topic of the next chapter. Her leadership made England strong, however, she did not have any children before her death, giving her the nickname - the virgin queen. Without any children, there were no heirs to the throne, and in 1603, the Tudor Era would come to an end.

AGE OF EXPLORATION

The Age of Exploration was a period during the Renaissance when European explorers sailed the seas to discover new lands and trade routes. Christopher Columbus and Vasco da Gama were two famous explorers of this time. The Age of Exploration advanced technology and navigation, increased international trade and helped to expand European influence around the world and laid the foundation for many of the global connections and interactions we see today. However, the encounters with native populations were often marked by conflict and exploitation of them and their land.

Age Of Exploration

Christopher Columbus

Christopher Columbus, who was born in Italy, was the first to sail across the world, looking for new trade routes to Asia. After pleading with the monarchy of Spain, they gave him three ships Nina, Pinta, and Santa Maria. His first voyage was in 1492, and he had discovered land. In October 1492, at 2 in the morning, he was awakened by a crewmate to a sighting of land. This land was the island of the Bahamas, a caribbean country, for which Christoper Columbus named "San "Salvador" meaning "Holy Savior". His first voyage also discovered other caribbean islands such as Cuba and Hispaniola. Columbus explored the land and met the indigenous people who lived there. He called them "Indians" because all that time, he thought he had reached India. Columbus thought he had found a new route to India, but he unknowingly discovered a whole new continent! He voyaged 3 more times to similar areas around the Caribbean, Central America in modern-day Mexico, Panama and Costa Rica, as well as the northern part of South America. Christopher's discoveries would ultimately open the doors for exploration by others.

I've Found India!

His whole life, Christopher Columbus was convinced that he had found India and a general shortcut to Asia, right until the day he had died.

I've Actually Found India!

Vasco da Gama was a Portuguese explorer who sailed around the southern tip of Africa and on to India, opening up a new sea route to Asia and establishing Portuguese dominance in the Indian Ocean trade.

Before Vasco da Gama, Europeans had to travel overland to reach Asia, which was very difficult and dangerous. But da Gama had the idea to sail around Africa and across the Indian Ocean to reach Asia, which was much faster and safer. He led the first expedition to do this and it was a huge success! He and his crew arrived in India in 1498, 6 years after Columbus' first voyage, and were able to trade with the people there, which made Portugal very wealthy. Vasco da Gama's accomplishment was important because it established a sea route to Asia that was controlled by the Portuguese. This allowed Portugal to dominate the Indian Ocean trade and become a major power in

Europe. It also opened up new trade opportunities and made it possible for other European countries to reach Asia by sea.

Thats The Name

Christopher Columbus' legacy can be seen throughout the world, particularly when it comes to names. For example, a province of Canada called British Columbia, the country in South America called Colombia and the capital of the USA, Washington D.C. is located in the District of Columbia, all named after Christopher Columbus.

Brazil

Two years after Vasco do Gama, another Portuguese explorer, Pedro Alvares Cabral, went to look for India. He was sent on a mission by the Portuguese king to find a new route to India, but he ended up discovering Brazil by accident! He was sailing westward across the Atlantic Ocean and veered off course, eventually sighting land that turned out to be Brazil, which is south of Columbus' route to the Caribbean. This was a very important discovery because it led to the colonization of Brazil by the Portuguese, and a new Portuguese land in the Americas

Around The Globe

Just over 20 years later, another Portuguese explorer called Ferdinand Magellan, sailed for Spain with five ships and a crew of about 250 men. They sailed across the Atlantic Ocean to South America and then traveled south to find a way through the continent. They discovered a passage, between South America and Antarctica, which was very dangerous as the waters were always choppy and the wind was always strong. Despite this, Magellan and his crew pushed forward and eventually sailed into the Pacific Ocean and all the way across this ocean and reached the Philippines, an island nation in Asia. There, Magellan clashed with the local people was killed in a battle. But his crew continued on and eventually made it back to Spain, completing the first circumnavigation of the world!
Magellan's accomplishment was very important because it proved that the world was round and that it was possible to sail all the way around it, and help Spain dominate global trade.

Francis Drake

With Spain and Portugal currently dominating the exploration of the world, other countries in Europe wanted to get involved, particularly England, France and the Netherlands. Drake is known for being the first Englishman to sail around the world. He set sail on this voyage in 1577 with five ships and a crew of around 160 men. They sailed around the southern tip of South America, across the Pacific Ocean, and then around the Cape of Good Hope in Africa. It was a very long and difficult journey, but they eventually made it back to England in 1580, becoming the second group of people to complete a trip around the world after Magellan's crew.

Drake was also known for his skill as a sailor and his daring exploits on the high seas. He was a privateer, which means that he was authorized by the English government to attack and capture enemy ships during times of war. He was very successful at this and became very wealthy as a result. Because privateering was so profitable, more and more sailors began to do it, leading up to Golden Age Of Piracy, an era that inspired the movie Pirates Of The Caribbean and more.

America!

Amerigo Vespucci was a famous Italian explorer who lived during the Age of Discovery. He was born in Italy in the 15th century and explored South America and the West Indies. When the European explorers first arrived in the Americas, they did not realize that they had discovered new continents. They thought that they had landed in Asia, and they called the land "the Indies." However, Vespucci realized that this was a new and unknown land Vespucci's first name is important because it was given to the new continents of North and South America!

Speaking French In Canada?

Jacques Cartier was a French explorer who lived during the 16th century and explorer of what is now Canada, where he claimed much of the land for France. Whilst, searching for a passage to Asia, he sailed north of where Columbus sailed, and found a passage, now known as the Lawrence River, which unfortunately did not lead him to Asia. However, his legacy lives on as he founded Quebec City and Montreal, which today are major cities in Canada, and is a reason why part of Canada is French speaking!

Age Of Exploration

The First Settlement

Walter Raleigh was an English explorer, poet, and writer who lived during the 16th and 17th centuries. He helped with the establishment of the Roanoke Colony, which was one of the first English colonies in North America. Raleigh sponsored several expeditions to the area that is now the coast of North Carolina, and he helped to establish a settlement on Roanoke Island in 1585. Although the settlement did not last long, it paved the way for future English colonies in North America.

Oceania

James Cook was a British explorer and navigator who lived during the 18th century. He is known for his exploration of the Pacific Ocean and the discovery of several islands and territories, such as Australia, New Zealand, and Hawaii.
Cook's most significant discovery was the eastern coast of Australia. In 1770, Cook set sail on the HMS Endeavour and landed in what is now known as Botany Bay. He claimed the land for Britain and named it New South Wales. This event led to the colonization of Australia by the British.

Cook is also remembered for his voyages to the Pacific, during which he discovered several islands and territories, including Hawaii, which he named the Sandwich Islands. He was the first European to visit many of these places and his voyages helped Europeans understand the Pacific. Cook would unfortunately be killed after attempting to kidnap the king of Hawaii in retaliation for them stealing one of his longboats.

Trade Wars

Initially, these voyages aimed to set up trade routes, where European countries would trade with lands in Asia, Africa and America. The European countries would gain new and exotic products never seen before such as tomatoes, potatoes, vanilla, tobacco and cocoa and America would gain never before seen products such as coffee, sugar, mango, banana and wheat. However, as the age of discovery continued, European countries started to exploit foreign lands and claim the land for themselves, starting the process of colonization that would put Europe in control of most of the world, until the process of decolonization began after World War 2.

Pirates Of The Caribbean

Pirates were a common sight during the Age of Discovery, and many of them were actually privateers who were commissioned by European governments to attack ships from other countries. The Golden Age of Piracy was a period in history, roughly from the late 17th century to the early 18th century, when piracy was at its peak in the Caribbean and other parts of the world. It is called the "Golden Age" because it was a time when pirates became very powerful and wealthy. During this time, pirates would get bounties (large money rewards) for were notorious for attacking ships and stealing treasure. They would often sail in small, fast ships called "pirate ships" that were equipped with cannons and other weapons. Pirates were known for their colorful flags and symbols, such as the skull and crossbones, which struck fear into their victims.

Blackbeard

Blackbeard was a notorious pirate who lived during the Golden Age of Piracy in the early 18th century. His real name was Edward Teach, but he is better known by his pirate nickname, Blackbeard. He was called

Blackbeard because he had a thick, black beard that he would sometimes braid and tie with ribbons.

Blackbeard was a fierce and intimidating pirate who was known for his cunning and ruthless tactics. He commanded a pirate ship called the Queen Anne's Revenge, which was a fast and heavily armed vessel. He used his ship and crew to attack and loot other ships, especially those that were carrying valuable cargo.

Blackbeard was famous for his appearance, as he would often wear a long, black coat and a big, black hat with a plume of feathers. He also carried several weapons, including pistols, knives, and a cutlass. To intimidate his enemies, he would light fuses in his beard, creating a smoky and terrifying effect.

Despite his fearsome reputation, Blackbeard was also known for his intelligence and charisma. He was able to gain the loyalty of his crew and maintain control over them.

RENAISSANCE

The Renaissance was a time of great change and creativity in Europe that lasted from the 14th to the 17th century. Major events included the invention of the printing press and the discovery of the Americas. Famous artists, writers, and thinkers such as Leonardo da Vinci, William Shakespeare, and Galileo Galilei emerged during this time. The Renaissance was a period of innovation and exploration that continues to inspire people today.

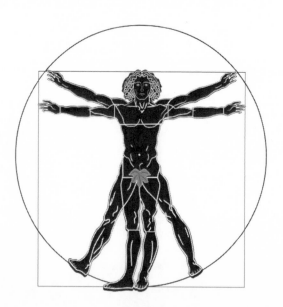

Renaissance

Born Again

The word "Renaissance" is a fancy way of saying "rebirth" in French. During the Renaissance period, people in Europe were interested in learning about new things and exploring different ideas. They were inspired by the culture of ancient Greece and Rome and wanted to bring back, literally rebirth, some of the ideas and knowledge from those times.

Florence

Florence, Italy was a very important city for art and culture during the Renaissance. Many famous artists, writers, and thinkers lived and worked in Florence during this time, and they created some of the most beautiful and famous artworks in history. Being an artist in Florence was very well paid, since there were wealthy patrons - people who paid artists - such as The Medici family. These artists include Leonardo da Vinci, who painted the Mona Lisa and The Last Supper and Michelangelo, who sculpted the David statue and painted the Sistine Chapel ceiling.

This Book Is Made Possible Thanks To...

the Renaissance. During the Era, the printing press, which allowed people to produce publications such as books in large quantities, was invented. Before, books were handmade, and were expensive. However, with this invention, books became much cheaper, a large number of people could access them and information could spread more quickly, a similar effect to how the internet is for us today.

To Be Or Not To Be

William Shakespeare was a famous writer who was born in 1564 in the Renaissance in England and is often called the greatest playwright in history. Shakespeare wrote many plays that are still performed and enjoyed today, like Romeo and Juliet, Hamlet, and Macbeth.

Shakespeare was known for his great storytelling skills and for using beautiful language and writing poetry. Many of his plays are about love, tragedy, and history. Sayings used today, such as "all's well that ends well" and "break the ice" originated from Shakespeare's work.

Backwards Notes

Leonardo da Vinci was a very talented man who lived during the Renaissance period. He was not only an artist, but also an inventor, scientist, and musician. He was interested in many different things and liked to explore new ideas. He created many beautiful paintings, such as the Mona Lisa and The Last Supper, but he also had many other talents. For example, he designed flying machines and studied how birds fly, and he created detailed drawings of the human body to better understand how it works.

One interesting fact about Leonardo da Vinci is that he wrote his notes backwards so that no one else could read them easily. He wrote from right to left, using mirror writing, which meant that his handwriting could only be read if it was held up to a mirror. Some people think he did this because he wanted to keep his ideas secret, but others think he did it because he was left-handed and it was easier for him to write this way.

Mona Lisa

The Mona Lisa is a famous painting created by Leonardo da Vinci during the Renaissance period. It is a portrait of a woman, who is believed to be a wealthy merchant's wife named Lisa. Leonardo used a special technique called sfumato, which means "smoky" in Italian, to create a soft, hazy effect in the painting. This gives the painting a very lifelike quality, and it makes the woman in the painting look like she is almost alive.

This technique, coupled by the unknown meanings gives the Mona Lisa painting a price tag of over $100 million today! Imagine what you could do with $100 million! Unfortunately for Leonardo, the painting only got this expensive after he died. Today, the Mona Lisa is on display in the Louvre Museum in Paris, France, where many people can come to see it every day.

Cutlery

In the renaissance, the people started using forks to eat food instead of their hands.

Questioning The World Around You

The Renaissance Era was all about questioning the world. Literature wasn't just about religion, and it started to explore love, nature and other topics, as we saw with Shakespeare. In science, again people began to question what religion said about the world and used observation and experimentation to challenge popular thought. This led to many important discoveries and advancements in science, such as Galilei Galileo's studies of the planets, Nicolaus Copernicus' theory of the Earth not being the center of the universe, Johannes Kepler discovering that planets move around the sun and Isaac Newton's laws of motion. Art was also influenced, and Renaissance art featured more lifelike depictions of events, as opposed to Middle Age art. The Renaissance and the curiosity it sparked also started an era of exploration, where people would begin to travel out more, particularly by sea to find new routes, which sparked the Age of Discovery as you will see.

INDUSTRIAL REVOLUTION

The Industrial Revolution was a period of time when people made many important inventions and changes that had a significant impact on how we live and work today. Some of the most important inventions included the steam engine, spinning jenny, and cotton gin, which helped increase productivity and efficiency in various industries. However, the growth of factories and urban areas also led to poor working conditions for many people. Despite these challenges, the Industrial Revolution transformed the world and laid the foundation for many of things we enjoy today.

Seeing In The Dark

Before the light bulb was invented by Thomas Edison, people had to rely on candles, lanterns, or gas lamps to see in the dark. This made it difficult to work or study after sunset, particularly in a large building such as a factory, because the light was often dim and flickering. However, the light bulb changed all of that.

The light bulb was a new type of lamp that used electricity to produce light. It was much brighter and more reliable than other types of lighting, which made it possible for people to work and study after dark. This was especially important for people who worked long hours and needed to get things done in the evening.

Thanks to the light bulb, people could read books, work on projects, or just spend time with their families after the sun went down.

Nettle Shirt

Since cotton was so expensive, most people in this era wore Hemp or Nettle (yes, from the stinging nettle!) clothing, which tended to be cheap, soft and lightweight. Nettle clothing slowly got replaced as cotton became less expensive over time.

Industrial Revolution

Fancy a job at the steam works?

Many factories were built in cities and towns all over the world. These factories needed workers to operate the machines and produce goods, and children were often hired to do this work.

Children as young as 5 or 6 years old were employed in factories, and they would work long hours, sometimes 12 hours a day or more. They would often work in dangerous conditions, with machines that could crush or cut off their fingers or limbs. There were no safety regulations or laws to protect them from harm, and many children were injured while working.

The children who worked in factories were usually from poor families who needed the extra income. They were paid very little, often just a few cents a day, and they had to work hard to earn even that. They had no time to play or go to school, and their health suffered because of the long hours and poor conditions.

Thankfully, over time, people began to realize that it was wrong and laws were passed to protect children from dangerous work, and schools were established to ensure that children could get an education instead of having to work.

Industrial Revolution

Migration

The Industrial Revolution caused urbanization. Before, people would live on farms and small villages, but as factories were being built, people from rural areas moved to the cities to work in them. They were attracted by the promise of higher wages and a chance for a better life. This meant that cities grew quickly, and they became crowded with people and buildings. People would often have to live in small, cramped apartments because there wasn't enough space to build houses. This meant that families had to live together in one room, and they often had to share a bathroom with many other people. The housing would often be cold and damp and diseases could easily be spread. Thankfully, for most people, working in the factories did improve their lives, but others were left with difficult times.

Steam Power

The Industrial Revolution was a time when many new machines and inventions were created that changed the way people lived and worked. It started with the Scottish inventor, James Watt, who was a brilliant engineer and inventor, who invented an improved version of the steam engine. Before Watt's invention, steam engines were not very efficient, and they were not widely used. Watt thought hard about how it could be improved and experimented around, using trial and error at first with little success. Eventually, his work paid off and he successfully made several improvements to the steam engine, including the use of a separate condenser, which made it much more efficient and allowed it to be used in transport and production.

Because of Watt's steam-powered engine, several other important inventions were made using the engine. These included:

The spinning jenny - it allowed people to spin multiple threads of yarn at the same time, making it faster and easier to make textiles like clothes and blankets.

The power loom - made it possible to weave textiles much more quickly and efficiently than before. The cotton gin: This machine was invented to help separate the seeds from cotton fibers, which made it possible to process cotton more quickly and efficiently.

On top of these production machines, Watt's steam engine was also able to be used in a steam train, therefore starting the age of rail transport. His inventions would make him a wealthy man!

To Good Health

During the Industrial Revolution, many factories were built in cities and towns, and they produced a lot of pollution. Smokestacks billowed out thick clouds of smoke and ash, which made the air dirty and difficult to breathe.

Despite the obvious drawbacks, some people believed that the pollution from factories was actually good for their health. They thought that the smoke and dust in the air could help to ward off diseases like tuberculosis and cholera, which were common at the time.

In reality, the pollution from certain factories was actually very harmful to people's health, and it caused many people to get lung and breathing problems and other illnesses, who were healthy before. People who worked in the factories were especially vulnerable to these health problems, because they were exposed to the pollution for long periods of time, but unfortunately, it would take a while before the public was made aware of the health issues and government made new rules.

AMERICAN REVOLUTION

The American Revolution was a war fought by the American colonies against Great Britain from 1775 to 1783. The colonists (Americans) were angry at the British government and fought for their independence. The war included famous battles like the Battle of Bunker Hill and was led by figures like George Washington and Paul Revere. The signing of the Declaration of Independence in 1776 declared the colonies as independent states, and the war ended with the signing of the Treaty of Paris in 1783, recognizing the United States as a new nation.

A New Nation Is Born

The Declaration of Independence is a document that declared the thirteen American colonies to be independent states and no longer a part of the British Empire. It was drafted by Thomas Jefferson, with input from other Founding Fathers such as John Adams and Benjamin Franklin, and was approved by the Continental Congress on July 4, 1776. The signing of the Declaration of Independence marked a turning point in the American Revolution, as it signaled the official break from British rule and the birth of a new nation. Independence Day is celebrated annually on July 4th in the United States to commemorate the signing of the Declaration of Independence.

Make Me A Tea

The Boston Tea Party was a significant event in the lead-up to the American Revolution. It occurred on December 16, 1773, in Boston, Massachusetts, and was a direct protest against the British Parliament's Tea Act, which had created a tax on tea imported into the colonies.
A group of colonists, including members of the Sons of Liberty, dressed up as Native

Americans to disguise themselves and boarded three British ships that were carrying tea. They then proceeded to dump the tea into the Boston Harbor, destroying 342 chests of tea, worth about $1 million in today's currency. This protest would further add to the tensions between colonists and Britain.

Yankee Doodle

The nickname "Yankee Doodle" was originally an insult used by the British to mock the American colonists, but the colonists eventually adopted it as a symbol of their pride and independence.

Founding Fathers

The Founding Fathers were a group of men who helped create the United States of America. They were important leaders who played a key role in the American Revolution, the war that led to America's independence from Great Britain.

Some of the most famous Founding Fathers include George Washington, Thomas Jefferson, Benjamin Franklin, and John Adams. These men were known for their bravery, intelligence, and dedication to the cause of freedom.

The Founding Fathers worked together to

create important documents like the Declaration of Independence and the United States Constitution, which established the framework for the new nation. They believed in ideas like democracy, freedom, and the rule of law, and they wanted to create a government that would protect these values.

Star-Spangled Banner

The first flag of the United States had 13 stripes, representing the 13 colonies, and 13 stars, representing each state. Because of this, it has been modified several times and today has 50 stars, one for each state.

George Washington

George Washington was a crucial figure in the American Revolution and played a significant role in the founding of the United States. He was a military leader, a statesman, and the first President of the United States.

During the Revolutionary War, Washington was appointed as the commander-in-chief of the Continental Army. He led the American forces against the British and was instrumental in securing a victory for the colonies.

Washington was known for his bravery,

strategic thinking, and his ability to inspire his troops.

Under Washington's leadership, the Continental Army won several important battles, including the Battle of Trenton and the Battle of Princeton. Despite facing many challenges, including a lack of resources and a poorly trained army, Washington was able to rally his troops and secure crucial victories that helped turn the tide of the war.

Thomas Jefferson

Thomas Jefferson was a Founding Father of the United States and played an important role in the American Revolution. He is most famous for writing the Declaration of Independence, which he wrote in just 17 days and was adopted by the new nation of the USA on July 4, 1776.

Jefferson believed that all people should have the right to life, liberty, and the pursuit of happiness, and he worked tirelessly to ensure that these ideas were enshrined in the founding documents of the United States.

Benjamin Franklin

Benjamin Franklin was an important diplomat and traveled to Europe to seek support for the American cause.

In France, Franklin became a popular figure and used his charm and intelligence to persuade the French to provide military and financial support to the American Revolution. He secured a useful partnership with France, which helped the Americans win the war against the British. Franklin also helped draft the constitution and secured his spot as one of the founding fathers.

Just The Beginning...

The Revolutionary War ended with the signing of the Treaty of Paris in 1783. The United States began as 13 states on the East Coast, with the remainder of the U.S. as we know it today still as colonies of other countries, or native american land. Over time, the U.S. expanded west, gaining territories and making the U.S. larger and larger. For example Texas would only become part of the U.S. in 1845, and California would only become part of the U.S. in 1850, over 80 years later from the declaration of independence.

NAPOLEONIC WARS

The Napoleonic Wars were a series of battles that took place in Europe between 1803 and 1815, named after Napoleon Bonaparte, a French military leader who became Emperor of France. The wars began with France declaring war on several European countries, leading to many battles fought on land and at sea. Some major events included the Battle of Trafalgar, where the British Navy defeated the French Navy, the invasion of Russia in 1812, where Napoleon's army suffered a devastating defeat, and the Battle of Waterloo, where Napoleon was finally defeated.

Trafalgar

The Battle Of Trafalgar was a big sea battle between the British navy and the French and Spanish navies. The battle took place near a place called Cape Trafalgar, which is in the south of Spain.

The British navy was led by a brave and famous admiral named Horatio Nelson, who had only one eye and one arm! He was a great leader and had won many battles before. The French and Spanish navies were led by a man named Admiral Villeneuve, who was very nervous because he knew that Nelson was a tough opponent.

The battle started when the two sides came together in a big line. The ships fired their cannons at each other, and there was lots of smoke and noise. The British navy was very well-prepared and had lots of good tactics, while the French and Spanish navies were not as organized.

During the battle, Horatio Nelson gave a famous order to his sailors: "England expects that every man will do his duty!" This inspired his sailors to fight bravely and they ended up winning the battle, even though Nelson was killed in the fight. The British navy captured lots of French and Spanish ships, and the victory helped Great

Britain to maintain their dominance of the seas. Today, Trafalgar Square is a place in London, and in the middle lies Nelson's column.

HMS Pickle

At the Battle of Trafalgar, the British navy had a ship called the HMS Pickle, which was a tiny ship used to carry messages between other ships!

War Tactics

During the Napoleonic Wars, which lasted from 1803 to 1815, many new military tactics and strategies were developed and improved. One of the most important developments was the use of artillery. Before, artillery was not widely used in battles, but during the wars, it became a crucial element of warfare. Artillery was used to fire bombs into enemy positions and create openings in their lines. This allowed soldiers to advance and take the enemy's position. Hot air balloons were also used by France to spy on enemy armies and formations.

In another way, soliders were usually deployed in a single line, but during the wars, new formations such as "column" formation were developed that allowed Napoleon's army to win many battles.

Napoleonic Wars

A Grand French Empire

Napoleon lead France to it's greatest size after the Battle Of Borodino, located in Russia in 1812. With this French Victory, France controlled Moscow, western Russia and much of mainland Europe, which was about the size of the USA! France owned Moscow for 36 days, before the French began to retreat.

Napoleon Bonaparte

Napoleon was actually short for a Frenchman at 5 feet 7 inches, but he was above average height for his time. His favorite horse was named Marengo, after his victory at the Battle of Marengo in 1800.

The Final Battle

After suffering from several defeats, Napoleon was forced into exile in 1814 to the birthplace of the island of Elba, where he was kept under close surveillance. Despite this, he managed to escape and returned to France, where news of his return would be welcomed, and he was able to form a new army. He would march his army to fight the final battle for France, the Battle of Waterloo. It happened in the year 1815 and was a big land battle between the armies of

France and a group of other countries, including Britain, Belgium, and the Netherlands.

The French army was led by Napoleon and the other countries were led by Duke of Wellington, who was a very experienced British commander and a master of strategy. The battle started when the two armies came together in a big field and started firing their weapons.

The French army was very strong and almost won the battle, but the Duke of Wellington was very clever and had a surprise trick up his sleeve. He hid some soldiers behind a hill and then surprised the French army by attacking them from behind. This turned the tide of the battle and the other countries ended up winning.

After the battle, the Duke of Wellington said a famous quote: "It was a close-run thing. The nearest run thing you ever saw in your life." This means that the battle was very close and could have gone either way. As a result of the French defeat, Napoleon was permanently removed from power in France, just 100 days after his return, and the French Empire would no longer exist.

VICTORIAN ERA

The Victorian Era was a period of time in England that lasted from 1837 to 1901, during the reign of Queen Victoria. It was a time of great change and innovation, as well as challenges and struggles.

Some of the major events that happened during this time included the Industrial Revolution, which brought about new technologies and ways of life, and the growth of the British Empire, which expanded England's influence around the world. There were also significant social and political movements, such as the women's suffrage movement, which fought for women's rights and the abolitionist movement, which worked to end slavery.

The Victorian Era was also a time of great literature, with famous authors such as Charles Dickens, Jane Austen, and the Bronte sisters creating stories that continue to be beloved today. The era is also known for its distinctive fashion, with women wearing long dresses and men sporting top hats and waistcoats.

The First Zoo

During the Victorian Era, a new and exciting attraction was introduced to the people of London - the zoo! The London Zoo was the very first public zoo in England, and it opened its doors in 1828. This was a time when people didn't have access to TV or the internet, so visiting the zoo was a thrilling experience that allowed them to see exotic animals from all over the world. The zoo was located in Regent's Park, which was a beautiful and spacious park in the heart of London. People could see all kinds of animals there, from big cats like lions and tigers to monkeys, birds, reptiles, and even elephants! It was a popular attraction for families, who could spend a day walking around the park, looking at the animals, and learning about them from the zookeepers.

Ping Pong

The game of table tennis, also known as ping pong, was invented during the Victorian Era as a way for people to play tennis indoors.

Victorian Era

Sherlock

During the Victorian Era, a famous detective named Sherlock Holmes was created by an author named Sir Arthur Conan Doyle. Sherlock Holmes is a fictional character who solves mysteries and crimes in London, England with his friend and sidekick Dr. Watson.

Flush The Toilet

During the Victorian Era, a very important invention was created that revolutionized the way people used the bathroom - the flushing toilet! Before this time, people would use chamber pots or outhouses, which were not very hygienic or convenient. But with the invention of the flushing toilet, people could go to the bathroom more easily and in a much cleaner way. The flushing toilet was actually invented in 1596, but it became common in the Victorian Era.

Say Cheese!

Era, a new way of capturing images was invented that changed the world - photography! Before this time, people had to rely on artists to create portraits or paintings of themselves or their loved ones. But with the invention of photography, people could capture an exact image of themselves or anything else they wanted to preserve.

The first successful photograph was taken by a man named Louis Daguerre in 1837.

The Story Of A Famous Storyteller

Charles Dickens was a very famous author who lived during the Victorian Era. He wrote many famous books, such as "Oliver Twist," "A Christmas Carol," and "Great Expectations." But did you know that he had a very unusual habit that helped him write his stories?

Charles Dickens used to walk for hours every day, sometimes up to 20 miles, to clear his mind and get inspiration for his stories. He would often take long walks through the streets of London, observing the people and places around him, and then use what he saw as inspiration for his books.

In fact, some of the most famous scenes in Charles Dickens' books were inspired by his walks. For example, the spooky atmosphere of the London streets in "Oliver Twist" was inspired by Dickens' own experiences walking through the city at night.

Hello, hello!

Queen Victoria was the ruler of the United Kingdom during the Victorian Era, and as queen, she reigned for 67 years, the longest of any British monarch until that point. She was a very important person who had many responsibilities, but she also had a special friend who helped her relax and have fun - a pet parrot!

Queen Victoria had a pet parrot that she loved very much. The parrot's name was Coco and the Queen used to take her everywhere she went, even to important meetings! Coco was very well-behaved and would sit quietly on the Queen's shoulder, listening to everything that was going on.

The Queen loved her parrot so much that she even gave her a special room in her palace to live in. The room was filled with toys and treats for Coco to enjoy, and the Queen would visit her every day to spend time with her. Coco was a very smart parrot and could even mimic the Queen's voice!

London Underground

The first underground train system in the world was built in London in 1863, a line between Paddington and Farrindon in London, stopping at 6 stops in between. The "trains" back then were an open top wooden carriage dragged along by. asteam engine. On it's opening day, the Underground carried over 38,000 people!

Penny Farthing!

The penny-farthing bicycle was very different from the bikes we have today. It had a very large front wheel and a very small back wheel. The rider would sit high up on the bike, with their legs pedaling the front wheel to move forward.

At first, the penny-farthing was only used by very wealthy people who could afford to buy such an expensive bike. But eventually, it became more popular and people started using it for transportation and racing.

Riding a penny-farthing was not easy, and it took a lot of skill and practice to stay balanced on the high seat. Worse still, imagine falling from that height! But for those who could ride it, it was a lot of fun and a great way to get around.

Today, we have much more modern and comfortable bikes, but the penny-farthing is still remembered as an important invention from the Victorian Era.

AMERICAN CIVIL WAR

The American Civil War was a big fight that happened in the USA a long time ago. It was a battle between two groups of people: the Union (also called the North) and the Confederacy (also called the South). The North wanted to keep the country together and end slavery, while the South wanted to be independent and keep slavery. The North included places such as Philadelphia, New York and Chicago and the south included places such as Alabama, Mississippi and Georgia. The south was a lot more reliant on growing crops such as cotton than the north, and therefore having slaves was much better business for them.

The war started in 1861 and lasted for four long years, where in the end, the Union won and slavery was abolished.

The Start of The War

The Battle of Fort Sumter was the first military engagement of the American Civil War. It took place on April 12-14, 1861, at Fort Sumter, a federal fort located in the harbor of Charleston, South Carolina. At the time, South Carolina had seceded from the United States and had formed its own government, which the Union did not recognize as legitimate. The Confederacy, which had also formed its own government, saw Fort Sumter as a symbol of federal authority and demanded that Union troops leave the fort.

The Union refused to leave, and on April 12, Confederate forces under the command of General P.G.T. Beauregard began bombarding the fort. Union troops, led by Major Robert Anderson, returned fire. The battle continued for 34 hours, with both sides firing at each other from a distance. The Union eventually ran out of supplies and surrendered the fort to the Confederacy on April 14.

The Battle of Fort Sumter was significant because it marked the beginning of the American Civil War.

Gettysburg

The Battle of Gettysburg was a major turning point in the American Civil War that took place from July 1 to July 3, 1863, in and around the town of Gettysburg, Pennsylvania. It was one of the largest and bloodiest battles of the war, with an estimated 50,000 casualties on both sides.

The battle began when Confederate General Robert E. Lee led his army of 75,000 soldiers into Pennsylvania with the goal of drawing Union forces away from the Confederate capital of Richmond, Virginia. However, Union General George G. Meade's Army of the Potomac intercepted Lee's army at Gettysburg, and the two sides clashed in a three-day battle that involved fierce fighting and heavy casualties.

The battle was fought on three main fronts: Cemetery Hill, Culp's Hill, and Little Round Top. The Confederates made several unsuccessful attempts to break through the Union lines, and after three days of fighting, Lee's army was forced to retreat back to Virginia. The Battle of Gettysburg was a significant turning point in the war, as it marked the first time that Confederate forces had been decisively defeated on Northern soil.

It also led to President Abraham Lincoln's famous Gettysburg Address, in which he honored the fallen soldiers and emphasized the importance of preserving the Union.

Baseball, Anyone?

in 1862, when a group of Union and Confederate soldiers decided to put aside their differences and engage in a friendly game of baseball in the midst of a battle. The game reportedly took place on the banks of the Potomac River, near Harrison's Landing, Virginia, and was played with a makeshift ball and bat.

According to reports, the game was played with great enthusiasm and sportsmanship, with both sides cheering on the players and even engaging in friendly banter and trash talk. At one point, a Confederate player hit a home run that landed dangerously close to Union lines, causing the Union soldiers to scatter momentarily before returning to the game.

The game eventually ended in a tie, and the soldiers returned to their respective camps.

Freed

The Emancipation Proclamation was a very important document that was issued by President Abraham Lincoln during the Civil War. The document declared that all slaves in the Confederate States of America were now free.

Before the Emancipation Proclamation, many people in America owned slaves, which means they owned other people and could force them to work for no pay. This was a very bad thing, and many people thought it was wrong. During the Civil War, the Union Army was fighting against the Confederate Army, which wanted to keep slavery. President Lincoln knew that slavery was wrong, and he wanted to do something to help the enslaved people. Since the emancipation proclamation, it meant that if a slave ran away from their owner and made it to Union Army territory, they would be free! Lots of slaves attempted to escape their owners and make it to the north.

WORLD WAR ONE

World War 1, also called the Great War, was a big war that happened from 1914 to 1918. It involved many countries from all around the world, including some big ones like Germany, Britain, France, and the USA.

The war started when a man named Archduke Franz Ferdinand, who was a prince from Austria-Hungary, was assassinated by a group of people in Serbia. This event set off a chain reaction of alliances and fighting between different countries.

The war was fought on land, in the air, and at sea, and was called the world war because for the first time, called up the armies from nations worldwide, from Japan to South Africa.

In the end, the war ended with the UK, US, France, Italy and other Allies victorious.

Soccer

During World War 1, soldiers from different countries were fighting against each other. It was a time of great conflict and tension. But in 1914, on Christmas Day, something remarkable happened. In some parts of the war zone, soldiers from both sides put down their weapons and played soccer together! This happened because the soldiers were missing their families and feeling homesick. They were also tired of fighting and wanted a break. So, they decided to call a truce, which means a temporary pause in fighting, to celebrate Christmas. During the truce, they came out of their trenches and exchanged small gifts like cigarettes and food.

One of the most famous things that happened during the truce was a soccer match. Soldiers from both sides set up goals and played a friendly game of soccer.

Trenches

During World War 1, soldiers on both sides would dig long, narrow trenches in the ground to protect themselves from enemy fire. These trenches were like long ditches that were deep enough for soldiers to stand in and protect themselves from gunfire and artillery shells.

But living in the trenches was not easy. The conditions were very difficult, and soldiers had to deal with rats and lice that were everywhere. The rats would scurry around in the trenches, searching for food and sometimes even biting the soldiers. The lice would live in the soldiers' clothing, making them very itchy and uncomfortable.

To make matters worse, the trenches were often wet and muddy. Soldiers would have to stand in the water for hours, and their feet would get soaked and cold. They would also have to deal with the smell of rotting food and dead bodies, which made the conditions in the trenches very unpleasant.

Trench warfare was a common theme in WW1 and was seen in most of the battles, such as the battle of Verdun, which lasted more than one year and the Bsttle of the Somme. Since trenches were secure and very difficult to infiltrate, the front lines during these battles didn't move much.

Red Baron

Manfred von Richthofen, also known as the "Red Baron," was a famous German fighter pilot during WW1. He is known as one of the greatest pilots in history because of his incredible skills and bravery in battle. The Red Baron flew a red plane, and was also known for his distinctive red uniform, which made him easy to spot in the sky. During the war, he he was best known for his Fokker Dr. I triplane. Throughout his career, the Red Baron shot down 80 enemy planes, but unfortunately, the Red Baron's luck eventually ran out. On April 21, 1918, he was shot down during a battle and died from his injuries.

A Noble Act

During World War 1, a British soldier named Henry Tandey fought in the Battle of Marcoing in France. During the battle, he came across a wounded German soldier and had a chance to shoot him, but he didn't. He chose to spare the soldier's life, and the soldier later crawled away.

Years later, after World War 1 had ended, Tandey became famous for his bravery in battle. However, it was not until much later that people realized the significance of his decision to spare the life of that German soldier. The wounded soldier that Tandey had spared was Adolf Hitler...

World War I

How Did The U.S. Get Involved?

At the beginning of WW1, the USA decided to remain neutral and not get involved in the war. However, as the war went on, the USA started to feel the effects of the conflict. German submarines were attacking American ships that were trying to deliver goods to other countries, and many Americans were upset about this. In 1915, Germany would sink the passanger ship RMS Lusitania, killing 1198 people, many of who were from the USA.

The final straw came in 1917 when the Germans sent a telegram to Mexico trying to convince them to attack the USA! This telegram, known as the Zimmermann Telegram, was intercepted by the British and shared with the Americans. The USA was angry by this and declared war on Germany in April 1917, helping the UK and France win against Germany and the Central Powers in 1918.

Spanish Flu

Towards the end of WW1, the Spanish Flu broke out in Kansas, USA and caused a global pandemic that would go to kill many more people than WW1. It was called the Spanish Flu because newspapers during the war reported of many cases in Spain!

WORLD WAR TWO

World War II was a major global conflict that took place from 1939 to 1945. It involved many countries from around the world, including the USA, Great Britain, Germany, Japan, and the Soviet Union.

The war started when Germany, led by Adolf Hitler, invaded Poland. This led to the involvement of other countries, including Great Britain and France, who declared war on Germany. The war then spread to other parts of Europe, with Germany quickly conquering many countries, including Denmark, Norway, Belgium, the Netherlands, and France.

The USA became involved in the war after the surprise attack on Pearl Harbor by Japan in December 1941. This led to the USA joining forces with Great Britain and the Soviet Union to fight against Germany, Japan, and their allies, who they defeated.

World War II

How Did It Even Start?

On September 1, 1939, Germany, led by Adolf Hitler, invaded Poland. The invasion caught the Polish military off guard, and Germany managed to capture half of Poland and make it part of Germany. Up until this point, Germany had been taking territory from other countries such as Austria and Czechslovakia. Since these lands were historically German, other countries tolerated Germany. Part of Poland was too historically German, but Poland had an alliance with France and the United Kingdom, and therefore these countries declared war on Germany when it attacked!

Secret Chess Code

The British government needed to send secret messages between military leaders, but they couldn't just use regular letters, because the enemy might intercept them. So they came up with a secret code called "Playfair," which was based on the game of chess! The code used a grid system and letter pairs to send messages that only the people who knew the code could read. It was really clever and helped the British keep their secrets safe.

Wotjek

During WW2, soldiers were often away from their families and loved ones for long periods of time. To help ease their loneliness and boost morale, some soldiers adopted pets to keep them company. These pets were often dogs or cats, but some soldiers even adopted more unusual pets, like a bear named Wojtek. Wojtek was a Syrian brown bear who was found by Polish soldiers in Iran. They took him in and cared for him, and he quickly became a beloved mascot of their unit. Wojtek became known for his strength, as he was able to carry ammunition crates that would normally require several men to lift. He was also known for his love of beer and cigarettes, which his soldier friends would sometimes give him as treats. Wojtek became a symbol of the Polish military and is still remembered today as a hero of WW2.

Hyper Soldiers

German soldiers and pilots were often given a stimulating drug called Pervitin to help them stay awake and alert during long missions. This drug today is known to be very addictive and comes with lots of side effects that can affect a person's thinking.

Rations

During World War II, many countries were affected by shortages of essential goods, including food and other everyday items. To make sure everyone had a fair share of these items, the government introduced a system called rationing. Rationing meant that people were only allowed to buy a limited amount of certain goods each week or month. This was to make sure that everyone had enough to eat and to prevent shortages from becoming too severe.

One of the items that was rationed in many countries, including the United Kingdom, was chocolate and other sweets. This meant that people could only buy a certain amount of chocolate or sweets each week, and they had to use ration coupons to do so. The rationing of chocolate was particularly hard for children, who loved sweets, but had to get used to the idea of not having them as often.

To make up for the lack of chocolate and sweets, people would often get creative and make their own treats using ingredients that were not rationed, such as fruits and nuts. Some children even made their own sweets, like toffee, using sugar and other ingredients that they could get their hands on.

Duped

The U.S. government had a clever idea to trick the Germans into thinking that they were going to invade France from a different location. They created a fake army and made it seem like it was a real army, with fake tanks, airplanes, and even fake soldiers! This operation was called "Operation Fortitude."

The idea behind the operation was to fool the Germans into thinking that the real invasion of France was going to happen in a different location than where it actually was. This would confuse the Germans and give the real invading army a better chance of success. To make the fake army seem real, the U.S. government used a variety of tricks and strategies.

For example, they built fake tanks out of wood and canvas, and placed them in strategic locations where the Germans would be able to see them. They also had airplanes fly over the area, dropping fake paratroopers to make it seem like the invasion was really happening. Meanwhile, the real invasion was happening in a completely different location, catching the Germans off guard.

Lottery

During World War II, many countries had conscription, which is also known as the draft. This meant that young men were required by law to serve in the military, whether they wanted to or not. In the USA the government held a draft lottery to determine which men would be called up for military service. Men who were drafted were given a notice to report for duty and had to leave their families and jobs to serve in the military.

Playing Cards

During World War II, many pilots were shot down behind enemy lines and had to navigate their way to safety. To help these pilots, the United States created special playing cards that had maps, survival tips and other useful information printed on them. These cards were given to pilots before their missions, so they could easily carry them in their pocket or survival kit.

The cards were designed to look like regular playing cards, with different suits and numbers on them. However, the cards also had hidden messages and codes that only pilots knew how to decipher.

29 Years

During WW2, Hiroo Onoda was a Japanese soldier who was sent to the Philippines to fight against the Allied forces. After the war ended in 1945, most Japanese soldiers returned home, but Onoda and a few other soldiers stayed behind and continued to fight. They believed that the war was still going on and that they had to continue fighting until they received orders to stop. Onoda and his fellow soldiers lived in the jungle for 29 years, surviving by foraging for food and avoiding contact with other people. They remained completely isolated from the rest of the world and did not know that the war had ended. They even engaged in small battles with local police and farmers who they believed were the enemy.

In 1974, Onoda was finally found by a Japanese college student who was searching for him. The student convinced Onoda that the war was over and that he needed to surrender. At first, Onoda did not believe him, but eventually he realized that the student was telling the truth.

Onoda surrendered to Philippine authorities, and his story made headlines around the world. He was hailed as a hero by many

Japanese people, who admired his dedication and loyalty to his country. Onoda returned to Japan and became a celebrity, but he struggled to adjust to life in modern society after spending so many years in the jungle.

Battle Of Normandy

The Battle of Normandy was a major battle during World War II that took place in the summer of 1944. It was also called the D-Day invasion, and it was a crucial turning point in the war.

The battle began on June 6, 1944, when the Allied forces invaded Normandy, a region in northern France that had been occupied by German forces. The Allied forces landed on five beaches along the coast. The invasion was planned in secret for months and involved a massive military operation, including naval and air support. The Allies had to overcome many obstacles, including German bunkers which were in advantageous locations, mines in the water, and bad weather. The invasion saw over 160,000 soliders cross the English Channel! Initially, it was not looking good as the Germans the advantage initially. However, through the determination of the army and the leaders to end the Nazis, the soliders slowly began to overturn the bunkers and after several long days of fighting, the soliders defeated the Germans, and for the first time in 3 years, the allies had access to mainland Europe, which up until that point was controlled by Germany. D-Day also helped pave the way for the eventual defeat of Nazi Germany.

I'll be out for a while mum

During World War II, many young boys wanted to fight for their country and be seen as heroes. One of those boys was Calvin Graham. He was just 12 years old when he decided to lie about his age and join the U.S. Navy in 1942.

At first, Calvin was assigned to a ship as a mess attendant, but he eventually transferred to the USS South Dakota, a battleship that was part of the Pacific Fleet. During his time on the ship, Calvin saw a lot of action. He manned a machine gun during several battles, including the Battle of Guadalcanal, where the South Dakota was hit by enemy fire.

Despite being in the middle of a war, Calvin managed to keep up with his studies and even completed eighth grade while onboard the ship. However, his time in the Navy was short-lived. In 1943, Calvin's true age was discovered, and he was discharged from the Navy. He was just 13 years old at the time.

Take that, Uncle.

During World War II, many people fought against Germany, however, it may surprise you to learn that one of Hitler's own family members actually fought against him - his nephew, William Patrick Hitler.

William Patrick Hitler was born in Liverpool, England, in 1911. His father, Alois Hitler Jr., was Adolf Hitler's half-brother. When William was a young man, he moved to Germany to try and benefit from his uncle's rise to power. However, he soon became frustrated with Hitler and his beliefs, and decided to leave Germany.

In 1939, William moved to the USA and eventually became a citizen. When World War II broke out, he enlisted in the U.S. Navy and was assigned to fight against his uncle's army.

William's actions helped to defeat the Nazi party that his uncle had led. After the war, he understandably changed his name to William Patrick Stuart-Houston and settled in the USA.

A clever man

Albert Einstein was a famous physicist who is best known for his groundbreaking theories of relativity. He was born in Germany but later moved to the United States to escape the persecution of Jewish people by the Nazis.

During World War II, Einstein noticed Germany unusually mining for Uranium and alerted the U.S. government that Germany was potentially developing an atomic bomb and that the U.S. should look into it. The U.S. agreed and began their own nuclear project, known as the Manhattan Project.

Einstein was known to be a brilliant scientist, and his work on nuclear physics had laid the groundwork for the development of atomic weapons, and indeed was invited to work on the Manhattan Porject.

However, despite his expertise, Einstein declined to participate, as was against war and the use of atomic weapons and did not want to contribute to their development. Nonetheless, the Manhattan Project was completed in 1945 and shortly after, two atomic bombs were dropped in Hiroshima and Nagasaki in Japan, abruptly ending the war, and making this time the only time nukes have ever been used in war.

Enigma

During World War II, communication between the military was very important, but it was also very secretive. The Germans had a code, called the Enigma code, which they used to communicate with each other. The code was very difficult to break, but the British government knew that if they could crack it, they could get important information about the German military's plans.

To help break the code, a team of scientists and engineers in the United Kingdom developed the world's first computer, called Colossus. The computer was huge and filled an entire room, but it was very advanced for its time. It used thousands of vacuum tubes, which were like light bulbs, to process information and help break the Enigma code. The team working on Colossus had to keep it a secret, even from their own government, because they didn't want the Germans to find out about it. They worked hard to improve Colossus and were eventually able to break the Enigma code, which helped the Allies win important battles.

Today, we have much smaller, faster and more advanced computers that can fit in our pockets, but Colossus was the first step in the development of modern computers. Without it, we might not have the technology we have today.

Churchill The Artist

Winston Churchill was not only a skilled politician and wartime leader, but he was also a talented painter. He began painting in his 40s and found it to be a relaxing and enjoyable hobby. He painted over 500 paintings throughout his lifetime, and many of them were exhibited in art galleries.

Smoking Is Bad

The Nazis were the first to create an anti-smoking campaign, not because they thought smoking was bad for health, but because they wanted to reduce the amount of tobacco that was imported from the United States.

CIVIL RIGHTS MOVEMENT

The Civil Rights Movement was a powerful movement that took place in the United States during the 1950s and 1960s. This movement aimed to end racism against African Americans, who had been treated unfairly for many years.

Some of the most important events in the Civil Rights Movement were the Montgomery Bus Boycott, the March on Washington in 1963, where Martin Luther King Jr. delivered his famous "I Have a Dream" speech and the Civil Rights Act of 1964 was another major milestone in the movement. This law made it illegal to discriminate against people based on their race, color, religion, or national origin. The Civil Rights Movement was a long and difficult struggle, but it paved the way for a more equal society.

Rosa Parks

Rosa Parks' refusal to give up her seat on a bus in Montgomery, Alabama on December 1, 1955 was a big moment in the Civil Rights Movement. At that time, segregation laws in the South required African Americans to sit in the back of the bus and give up their seats to white people if the white section was full. When the white section of the bus became full, the bus driver demanded that Rosa gave up her seat, but she refused. She ended up getting kicked off the bus, which sparked the Montgomery Bus Boycott that lasted for 381 days. African Americans in Montgomery boycotted the buses and organized carpools, walked or cycled to their destinations instead. The boycott was a major challenge to segregation laws and the bus companies lost a lot of money because of it. The boycott was led by Martin Luther King Jr., who emerged as a national leader during this time.
The Montgomery Bus Boycott spread nationwide, bringing civil rights to the public eye across the U.S. and inspired similar protests across the country.

Civil Rights Movement

Little Rock Nine

The Little Rock Nine were a group of nine African American students who were enrolled at Little Rock Central High School in Little Rock, Arkansas in 1957. At that time, racial segregation was still legal in many parts of the USA, and Little Rock Central High School had been an all-white school.

The integration of the school was ordered by the U.S. Supreme Court which ruled that segregation in public schools was illegal. The Little Rock Nine could attend the school because of their academic achievements, but their enrollment was met with resistance from many white residents of Little Rock.

On September 4, 1957, the first day of school, the Little Rock Nine attempted to enter the school, but were met with a hostile mob of protesters who were determined to prevent them from attending. The Governor Orval Faubus also ordered the National Guard to block the students' entry into the school, claiming that he was concerned for their safety. Despite all this, the Little Rock Nine remained committed to their cause and continued to attend the school and their bravery and determination helped to advance the cause of civil rights.

Civil Rights Movement

I Have A Dream

On August 28, 1963, Dr. Martin Luther King Jr. delivered his historic "I Have a Dream" speech at the Lincoln Memorial in Washington, D.C. during the March on Washington for Jobs and Freedom. This speech is considered one of the most iconic speeches in American history and a defining moment of the Civil Rights Movement.

The March on Washington was a massive political rally that brought together over 200,000 people from all over the country to advocate for civil rights and economic equality for African Americans. Dr. King was one of several civil rights leaders who spoke at the event, but his speech became the most memorable and impactful.

In his speech, Dr. King expressed his vision for a future where all people are judged by the content of their character, not the color of their skin. He spoke of the need for unity, and called for an end to discrimination and segregation.

Dr. King's powerful delivery captured the spirit of the Civil Rights Movement and inspired millions of people to join the struggle for justice and equality.

COLD WAR

The Cold War was a time of tension between two superpowers, the United States and the Soviet Union, that lasted from the end of World War II in 1945 until 1991.

Some major events during the Cold War include:

The Berlin Blockade (1948-1949) where the Soviet Union blocked off access to West Berlin, which was part of occupied Germany.

The Korean War (1950-1953): The Soviet-backed North Korea invaded South Korea, and the US and its allies came to South Korea's defense. The war ended in a stalemate, with North and South Korea still divided to this day.

The construction of the Berlin Wall (1961), Cuban Missile Crisis (1962) where a nuclear war was on the verge of breaking out,

The Vietnam War (1955-1975) and The fall of the Berlin Wall (1989): After years of tension and division, the people of East Germany were allowed to travel to the West for the first time in decades. This led to the eventual reunification of Germany, as well as being a key event that led to the and the end of the Cold War.

Cold War

Chilly!

The Cold War was called a "cold" war because it never involved direct military conflict between the United States and the Soviet Union, only indirect threats.

Berlin Blockade

After World War 2, Germany was split into sections, each being owned by the victors. The Soviet Union occupied East Germany, including half its capital, Berlin, and the west occupied the other half. This annoyed the USSR, because West Berlin was in the middle of USSR territory. To try and force the west out of West Berlin and control the whole city, the USSR blocked western access to West Berlin, meaning that it's population were starved of food and other supplies. The western nations were quick to react to the blockade by airlifting supplies to Berlin. These flights would have to go, whatever the weather, and the airlift was made more difficult as Soviet planes tried to interfere with the flight path. The Berlin airlift lasted over a year, and in total planes flew over 250,000 times carrying well over 3000 tons worth of supplies every single day. Beginning in 1948, the Berlin blockade was a major event that kickstarted the Cold War.

I Spy With My Little Eye

During the Cold War, the United States and the Soviet Union were in a state of and competition, and each side wanted to know as much as possible about what the other side was doing. So, both countries tried to spy on each other using all kinds of different methods, including using spy planes and other sophisticated technology. Spy planes are airplanes that are specially designed to gather secret information from other countries. The USA and the USSR both developed spy planes that were able to fly at high altitudes and take pictures of the ground below. These pictures could be used to gather information about military bases, factories, and other important locations. One of the most famous US spy planes was called the U-2, which was first developed in the 1950s. The U-2 was able to fly at an altitude of over 70,000 feet, which was much higher than any other airplane at the time. This made it very difficult for other countries to shoot it down or intercept its signals. The U-2 was used to gather secrets about the Soviet Union and other countries during the Cold War.

Vietnam

The Vietnam War was a long conflict that took place in Vietnam, a country in Southeast Asia, from 1955 to 1975. At the time, Vietnam was divided into two parts: North Vietnam, which was communist, and South Vietnam, which was non-communist.

The USA became involved in the Vietnam War because it wanted to stop the spread of communism in Southeast Asia. The US sent soldiers and supplies to South Vietnam to help them fight against North Vietnam and the communist Viet Cong guerrillas.

The war was fought in the jungles and cities of Vietnam, and it was very difficult for the US soldiers because they were fighting in a foreign country against an enemy that was very hard to see. The Viet Cong used guerrilla tactics, which means they would hide in the jungle and then attack the US soldiers suddenly and quickly. This made it very hard for the US to win the war.

The Vietnam War was also controversial in the USA. Many people did not support the war, and there were protests and demonstrations against it. In the end, the Vietnam War was a loss for the USA, and the communist North Vietnam took over the whole country.

The Soviet Union also developed its own spy planes, such as the MiG-25, which was able to fly at high speeds and altitudes. The MiG-25 was used to gather intelligence about the US and other countries during the Cold War.

Bay Of Pigs

When Fidel Castro came into power in Cuba, the US government tried to "overthrow" his government, which often meant assassinating him. They wanted this because he was a communist and since Cuba is close by to the USA, was a big threat during the Cold War. The resulting attempt was called the Bay of Pigs invasion, but this failed as the supposedly secret plan was found out by Cuba. Very awkward.

Join Us

The US government tried to use subliminal messaging to try to get Soviet citizens to defect to the West, by broadcasting messages from a radio station called "Radio Free Europe". The USSR had a propaganda campaign that involved sending a satellite called Cosmos 186 to orbit the Earth, which played patriotic music for anyone who could pick up its radio signal.

Nuclear War

During the Cold War, the threat of both sides using nuclear bombs was felt by everyone. A nuclear war would cause worldwide damage from the radiation and could even end life as we know it, and all was needed was for a button to be pressed to send a nuke off. One time in 1962, the world came close to nuclear war when a Soviet Submarine armed with a nuke was close to firing. Since they were underwater and had lost contact with the outside world, they thought the Cold War became physical. Therefore two officers in the submarine agreed to fire their nuke at a U.S. boat and pressed the activate button, but three buttons needed to be pressed. The final person, Vasily Arkhipov, refused to press the button, suggesting that they wait for an order to launch the nuke first, and the nuke was never launched. Vasily's actions that day saved the world.

A Race To Space

In 1957, the Soviet Union launched a small satellite called Sputnik into space. This was a really big deal because it was the first time a man-made object had been sent into orbit around the Earth! The satellite was just a metal ball with some antennae sticking out of it, but it was a major achievement for the Soviet Union.

The launch of Sputnik also had another important effect: it kicked off something called the "Space Race" between the US and the USSR. The Space Race was a competition between the two countries to see who could achieve the most impressive feats in space exploration. The US government was worried that the Soviet Union was becoming too powerful and too technologically advanced, and they didn't want to be left behind.

So, the US government launched their own space program to try to catch up with the Soviet Union. They started launching their own satellites and sending astronauts into space. In 1961, the Soviet Union sent the first man into space, named Yuri Gagarin. The US responded by sending their own astronaut, named Alan Shepard, into space just a few weeks later.

The Space Race continued throughout the 1960s and mostly ended after the U.S. became the first country to put a man on the moon in July 1969. This is when Neil Armstrong stepped onto the moon and said "this is one small step for man, but one giant leap for mankind".

Life On The Other Side

During the Cold War, the separation between the west and the east was called the iron curtain. If you were born on the other side of the Iron Curtain, life would be very different. The government controlled all of the factories and businesses, and people didn't have a lot of choice about what they could buy or where they could work. There were shortages of food, clothing, and other basic goods, and people had to wait in long lines just to get the things they needed. The government also controlled media and education, meaning that the channels on the TV, the films available and books and schools were very limited. The TV would also have a few government approved channels which were often political. Books and schools could not teach people about topics that the government has not yet first approved. Travelwas also restricted, and you would need to get permission from the government if you wanted to travel abroad! The government would often used spies to keep an eye on people. The secret police, such as the KGB in the USSR would monitor people's activities and conversations, and many people were afraid to speak out or do anything that might be seen as a threat to the government. Even choosing a job was mainly determined by the government, and you couldn't easily change job if you didn't like your current one.

A Divided City

The Berlin Wall was a wall that separated the city of Berlin in Germany into two parts during the Cold War. It was built in 1961 by the government of East Germany, which was a communist country. The purpose of the wall was to keep people from East Germany from going to West Germany, which was a non-communist country.

The Berlin Wall consisted of two outer walls made of concrete and was very tall. In between the walls were barbed wires, mines and guard towers with soldiers who would shoot anyone who tried to cross the wall. Many families were separated by the wall, and they were not able to see each other for many many years.

The Berlin Wall was a symbol of the division between the East and the West during the Cold War. It was a physical representation of the Iron Curtain that separated the communist countries of Eastern Europe from the non-communist countries of Western Europe.

Cold War

In 1989, after many years of tension between East and West Germany, the Berlin Wall was finally torn down, and people who have been separated can now see each other again. This was a very important event in history because it symbolized the end of the Cold War and encouraged other communist countries to open up. In 1991, two years after the wall fell, the Soviet Union collapsed under a civil war, and communism was mostly abolished, officially ending the Cold War and opening a new chapter for global cooperation.

Made in United States
North Haven, CT
25 May 2023

36983165R00112